THE SERPENT'S COIL
FARLEY MOWAT

"The serpent's coil? It is the symbol for 'cyclone,' and after reading this true story one could hardly forget it ... I found it the most stirring maritime writing since James Gould Cozzens' S.S. *San Pedro*."
—*San Francisco Chronicle*

"Mr. Mowat has caught the very mood and feeling of this unique episode in the annals of the sea. He tells his tale with the precision of a ship's log, and in the same hard and driving manner."
—*The New York Times Book Review*

"Not only is this a vivid picture of what men and ships undergo in such storms; it shows also the dangers and complications of rescue and salvage; it blends humor, suspense, and courage in its re-creation of the men who brought the ship through its ordeals."

—*Horn Book*

THE SERPENT'S COIL

Farley Mowat

Seal Books
McClelland and Stewart-Bantam Limited
Toronto

To the
seafaring men of
NEWFOUNDLAND
peers of the greatest mariners
who ever sailed the unquiet plains
of the
Western Ocean

THE SERPENT'S COIL
*A Seal Book / published by arrangement with
McClelland & Stewart Ltd.*

PRINTING HISTORY
*McClelland & Stewart edition published December 1980
Published as volume 2 of the author's Atlantic rescue 1980
Seal edition / October 1981
2nd printing . . . September 1983*

ISBN 0-7704-2098-2

*Seal Books are published by McClelland and Stewart-Bantam
Limited. Its trademark, consisting of the words "Seal Books"
and the portrayal of a seal, is the property of McClelland and
Stewart-Bantam Limited, 60 St. Clair Ave East, Suite 601,
Toronto, Ontario M4T 1N5, Canada. This trademark has been
registered in the Trademarks Office of Canada. The trademark
consisting of the word "Bantam" and the portrayal of a
rooster is the property of and is used with the consent of
Bantam Books, Inc., 666 Fifth Avenue, New York, New York
10103. This trademark has been duly registered in the Trademarks Office of Canada and elsewhere.*

PRINTED IN CANADA

U   11 10 9 8 7 6 5 4 3 2

FOREWORD

During the final days of 1951, hurricane winds in the North Atlantic savaged an ex-wartime Liberty freighter named *Flying Enterprise,* some three hundred miles southwest of Ireland. Abandoned by all except her Captain, and heeled over until she was virtually on her beam ends, *Flying Enterprise* held the world's attention during two bitter weeks while men fought desperately to save her. But on January 10th, 1952, the old sea took its victory and *Flying Enterprise* went down only forty miles from a safe port.

The ship was lost, yet her name still lives as a symbol of heroic endurance against wind and sea.

There is another vessel, also an ex-wartime Liberty, which has earned equal immortality. Her name is *Leicester,* and she is still alive after having survived a hundred-day ordeal which is without parallel in modern times. The story of her survival is not only the tale of a ship which would not die. It is, more vitally, the story of a handful of men who would not let her die.

My admiration for the quality of these men is unbounded, and I pray that I have done them justice in this book. I wish to thank them for enabling me to tell their tale. I also wish to acknowledge gratefully the wholehearted assistance of the shore people of Foundation Company of Canada who extended to me the kind of cooperation which writers dream about—and seldom find.

FARLEY MOWAT

From The Beaufort Scale of Wind Force

BEAUFORT NO.	SEA MILES PER HOUR (KNOTS)	SEAMAN'S DESCRIPTION	EFFECT AT SEA
0	—1	Calm	*Sea like a mirror.*
1	1-3	Light air	*Ripples with the appearance of a scale but without foam crests.*
2	4-6	Light breeze	*Small wavelets, more pronounced; crests have a glassy appearance and do not break.*
3	7-10	Gentle breeze	*Large wavelets. Crests begin to break. Foam of glassy appearance. Perhaps scattered white horses.*
4	11-16	Moderate breeze	*Small waves, becoming longer; fairly frequent white horses.*
5	17-21	Fresh breeze	*Moderate waves, taking a more pronounced long form; many white horses.*
6	22-27	Strong breeze	*Large waves begin to form; the white foam crests are more extensive everywhere.*
7	28-33	Moderate gale (high wind)	*Sea heaps up and white foam from breaking waves begins to be blown in streaks.*
8	34-40	Fresh gale	*Moderately high waves of greater length; edges of crests break into spindrift.*
9	41-47	Strong gale	*High waves. Sea begins to roll.*
10	48-55	Whole gale	*Very high waves with long overhanging crests. The surface of the sea takes a white appearance. The rolling of the sea becomes heavy and shocklike.*
11	56-66	Storm	*The sea is completely covered with long white patches of foam. Everywhere the edges of the wave crests are blown into froth.*
12	66+	Hurricane	*The air is filled with foam and spray. Sea completely white with driving spray.*

Note: The sea mile is 6080 feet, approximately 1.15 land miles.

PART ONE

CHAPTER 1

On the morning of August 28th, 1948, *Foundation Josephine* stood in to the Nova Scotian port of Halifax.

The fairway was full of ships that day. As *Josephine* drove in past Meagher's Beach she passed an aircraft carrier escorted by a cruiser, two immense tankers, and a 20,000-ton bulk-cargo vessel. Any of these should have dwarfed a ship of *Josephine's* dimensions to relative insignificance. But despite her modest size—she was barely two hundred feet in length and of only a thousand tons displacement—she had about her such an aura of concentrated power and such a sea-going presence that she easily held her own in comparison with the bigger ships.

Her high bows, throwing up a foaming bone across her teeth, gave her something of the go-to-hell look of a destroyer. There the resemblance ended. Her house and bridge were set well forward of amidships, while abaft the boat deck her hull fell away with startling suddenness to an elongated and wide-open after deck which seemed to lie almost on a level with the water. She gave the impression of rearing back on her heels like a thoroughbred filly, and the rake of her two masts and of her funnel increased the impression of latent power, held under a tight rein.

Her house and bridge shone brilliant white above a gloss-black hull, and the broad green band around her funnel added just the right touch of colour. Her flared bows and exaggerated sheer gave her the kind of womanly lines that seamen love.

The bone at her teeth diminished as she rounded the foot of George's Island and swung in toward the docks along Water Street. Her siren sounded stridently, and two fishermen at work on a moored long-liner looked up to watch her coming in.

"What kind of a boat do you call that anyway?" asked a loafer on the dock beside them.

The younger fisherman considered the question for a moment.

"I'd call that one a tug, sorrr," he said, in the soft Newfoundland drawl.

The loafer gave him a pained look.

"Hold on, now," he said reproachfully. "I know a tug-boat when I see one. Tugboats are little piddling things. That boat there looks like she'd be happy in mid-ocean in a hurricane."

The Newfoundlander grinned. "Yiss, sorrr. Indeed she would. And there's been a time or two when she's been out and it blowin' like the Bull of Barney and the nearest of land a t'ousand miles away."

"Ned's given you the rights of it," said the second fisherman, a native Nova Scotian. "She's what they call an ocean-rescue tug. A deep-sea boat—maybe the finest one there is. 'Course she *does* have a Newfoundlander crew, which counts against her just a mite. But she's fit to go anywhere, in the wust kind of weather—and that's just what she does."

Josephine came in toward her wharf with what seemed enough headway to carry her right over it and halfway up Water Street; then at the right moment her telegraph rang sharply, and under her low counter the dirty waters of the harbour boiled up brown as her 3200-horsepower diesels drove her immense bronze screw into reverse. The way came off her almost as quickly as if she had collided with some underwater object and, barely moving, she drifted alongside the wharf where a handful of men were waiting to take her lines.

On the wing of her low, curving bridge, her Master, Captain John Cowley, a stocky, dark-haired man with a well-worn naval officer's cap pulled firmly down over his eyes, watched while the lines were made fast. Then the telegraph signalled "Finished with engines." The deep vibration of the diesels dulled, and *Foundation Josephine* lay quiet. She did not give the impression of lying asleep, as most vessels do when they are moored. She still looked ready and alert.

Foundation Josephine was conceived in 1940. When the war began there was only a handful of salvage and rescue vessels available to the Allies, and the majority were designed primarily for work in coastal waters. Aided by these few coastal tugs, any ships which were attacked by submarines on the approaches to North America or to Europe—and which remained afloat—had some chance of survival. But ships which were hit while in mid-Atlantic had no chance at all.

A new type of salvage tug was clearly needed. What was required was a vessel of some size, which could endure the worst the North Atlantic might fling at her, and which could at the same time take hold of a crippled merchant ship of up to 15,000 tons dead weight and tow her at convoy speeds of 8 or 10 knots for distances as great as 1500 miles.

The British architect entrusted with the design of the new type of tug was given forty-eight hours to prepare a set of plans. The Scottish shipyard which was to have the order for the prototype vessel was given three months in which to build her.

The first of the new ships put to sea late in 1941. She was named *Bustler* and she gave her name to a class which eventually embraced seven deep-sea rescue ships. The third of the new ships was called *Samsonia*. When she put to sea for the first time, to accompany a Halifax-bound convoy in September of 1942, she was commanded by a quiet and unobtrusive man named John Cowley, Lieutenant Commander, Royal Naval Reserve.

Cowley and *Samsonia* remained together till the war was done. Evading submarine attacks and dodging bombs, they brought to port during those three years a score of ships which otherwise would have taken the long plunge into the Atlantic deeps.

At war's end, the special need for the new convoy tugs vanished overnight. One of them, *Turmoil*, was chartered by an English firm and later became world-famous during the salvage epic which centred around the *Flying Enterprise*. *Samsonia* caught the fancy of the Canadian salvage company, Foundation Maritime. But the Salvage Master and Marine Superintendent of that company, Captain Robert Featherstone, saw more than the tug herself: and when she set sail across the Atlantic under her new name, *Foundation Josephine*, she was still under the command of John Cowley.

Her passage over, in January of 1947, was a foretaste of things to come. Eight hundred miles off Newfoundland, a sea swept her end for end, carried away her antennae and damaged her radio installations. Her operator could receive on his emergency set, but he could not transmit.

On January 15th, *Josephine*'s Sparks (radio operators aboard most ships are known as "Sparks" or "Sparkie") heard a faint s o s. Unable to ask for detailed information, all he could tell Cowley was that the message appeared to have come from a laden British tanker, the *Fossularca*, which reported herself to be foundering. A few hours later, Sparkie picked up a second message giving the battered tanker's dead-reckoning position. It was 250 miles to the northeast, some 200 miles off the coast of Newfoundland.

By this time *Josephine* herself was in enough trouble to have kept any ordinary vessel, and her master, content to mind their own affairs. She had been swept a second time and one of her two lifeboats had been smashed to kindling. Her lobby was flooded, and she was leaking in a score of places. The temperature had dropped to well below freezing and the tug, half submerged most of the time, was icing so badly that her stability was threatened. The seas were running thirty to thirty-five feet high and the gale had registered wind speeds of 75 miles an hour. Cowley quietly weighed the chances. Then he gave the helmsman a new course.

Josephine swung quartering to the seas, rolling and pitching like a thing possessed. Slowly she worked her way into the driving scud and snow toward the helpless tanker.

She was two days on that passage. She reached the *Fossularca* on January 17th, and it was only by the modern miracle of radar that she found the smitten ship at all.

On the morning of January 20th a bunch of incredulous salvage men of Foundation Maritime stood on the docks in Halifax and watched an ice-shrouded tug and her elephantine tow easing their way up the harbour. *Josephine* had reached her new home port and had successfully completed her first salvage job in West Atlantic waters.

The success was not due solely to Cowley's skill, or to the indomitable qualities of *Josephine* herself. Apart from Cowley, Chief Engineer John Gilmour, and some others of the engine-room staff, the crew were all Foundation men who had gone over from Halifax to bring the new tug home.

They were mostly Newfoundlanders and in the days to come it was to be Newfoundlanders who would supply the nerve, bone and sinew—and not a little of the brains—which would help to make the name *Foundation Josephine* a byword on the North Atlantic shipping routes.

Between February of 1947 and early August of 1948, *Josephine* rescued, or took part in the rescue of, twenty-one ships. Thirteen of these were vessels which had suffered crippling damage at sea. Five were ships driven ashore on the rock-bound Canadian coasts which had to be repaired, pumped out and then refloated. One was a flaming collier adrift in narrow waters. And one was a huge tanker laden with aviation gasoline, which had to be beached, repaired, and then refloated after a collision.

Josephine had seldom been idle during her first year and a half under the house flag of Foundation Maritime, and by late August of 1948 she was beginning to show the strain. Robert Featherstone, the saturnine guiding genius of the company's salvage and rescue operations, had therefore decided to recall *Josephine* from her summer station at North Sydney, on the northeastern tip of Nova Scotia, and put her on drydock in Halifax for an overhaul and refit.

To replace *Josephine* in her watchdog role at North

Sydney, where she had been able to respond to s o s calls from both the open Atlantic and the Gulf of St. Lawrence, Foundation Maritime's second ocean-going tug, *Foundation Lillian*, was recalled from her normal station at Bermuda. Thus Featherstone ensured that when the autumn gales began to blow in early September, shipping on the western approaches to the continent would still have help at hand if help was needed.

CHAPTER 2

On the same day *Foundation Josephine* arrived in Halifax to begin her refit, a launch put out from Tilbury docks, some 2500 miles to the east of Halifax, and angled fussily athwart the murky waters of the lower Thames toward a merchant vessel anchored in the stream.

Captain Hamish Lawson, a solid, wind-worn man in the full vigour of his middle thirties, sat erect in the stern sheets of the launch, intent upon the looming bulk of a black-painted ship ahead of him. The tide was running home to the sea and the big vessel was tugging wilfully at her cables as London River sucked along her flanks where two battered scows lay tethered. From the ship's outswung cargo booms, clam buckets plunged with a run into the bellies of the scows. Winches rattled and steam hissed whitely in the late summer sun. Steel ropes came taut. The clams rose heavily, grey water dripping from between their iron teeth.

The ship was taking ballast—a sludge of sand and gravel dredged from the bottom of the river: the sediment of aeons, rank with the debris of all the ages since men first sailed their vessels down the Thames from London to the waiting sea.

Ballast—to lade an empty vessel so that she would take kindly to the waves. Ballast—to steady her during a voyage to some distant port where a lading of freight lay waiting.

The launch rounded the big ship's counter and Lawson glanced sharply up at the words painted along each side of the cruiser stern. White letters marched boldly over the black plates, proclaiming to the world that this was the *Leicester* out of London. Was it fancy, Lawson wondered, or could he see the outline of another name beneath the freshly painted words—the outline of a half-seen ghost . . . *Samkey*.

The launch bumped gently along the port quarter. Lawson scrambled up the dangling Jacob's ladder to gain the deck; and in that instant he ceased to be a rather nondescript fellow in a business suit and became the Master of a ship.

He made his way across the littered decks, stepping quickly over a pile of hatch boards, barely perceiving the ordered confusion of a vessel making ready for sea. Lawson entered the port alleyway and made his way to the Master's cabin, where he slung his dispatch case on the bunk and stripped off his shore-going jacket. Then, in clear defiance of his will, the name which lurked within his inner eye flickered and grew sharp once more.

Samkey.

Leaning his strong forearms on his built-in desk, Lawson gave his memory rein.

He remembered the November day in 1947, less than a year before, when he had sat comfortably in an office of the Federal Steam Navigation Company, contemplating the rubicund face of the Marine Superintendent. Outside, the winter rain beat coldly over London; but Lawson was aglow with a warmth no rain could chill, for crisp in his breast pocket were his newly issued papers as a foreign-going master in the merchant service.

"You'll understand, Captain," the Marine Superintendent had said, "that *Samkey*'s hardly a luxury vessel."

Lawson smiled. "When I left the Navy to take my ticket in the Merchant Service, I wasn't thinking of a Cunarder for my first peacetime command, you know. A Liberty will suit me fine."

And in truth Lawson was well suited. He knew the war-built Liberty ships well, having watched them in a hundred convoys, deep-laden with war cargoes outward bound from Canada for England. Ugly they may have been, and slow, and crude—but they were enduring ships. They could carry cargo and they could take punishment, whether from the sea or from the enemy.

On the following day, the two men drove down to Gravesend and there Lawson was introduced to his first civilian command. Four hundred and twenty feet in length, twin-decked; driven by a triple-expansion steam engine, and fired with oil, she was of 7600 tons gross register and about 10,000 tons capacity.

The two men went aboard. "She's one of about two hundred Liberties built on Lend Lease by Uncle Sam," the Marine Superintendent had explained, "I suppose that's why they all bore his name. Sam-this, Sam-that, Sam-damn near everything. In 1947 we bought this one and a sister ship for the run to North America and on to New Zealand and Australia. *Samkey* has only made one round trip out. You'll be taking her on her second voyage down under."

As it turned out, the Superintendent was wrong about that. Early in December, before he could actually assume command of her, Lawson was stricken with pneumonia. He was still convalescing when, on January 24th, *Samkey* let slip her lines and pointed her bows downstream, under command of another master, and bound for Cuba in ballast.

On January 31st, *Samkey*'s radio operator passed his daily position message to the owners via Horta Radio in the Azores. The ship was then following the low-powered steamer track toward the American Gulf ports. The radio operator reported moderate winds accompanying a very heavy sea—and that was all. His fist on the key, the voice of the ship, was never heard again.

For days thereafter the ether over the North Atlantic rang emptily to the call sign of *Samkey* as shore stations and the transmitters of other ships tried in vain to rouse her from her silence.

Search aircraft made several flights to and beyond her

last-reported position; they found no trace of the missing vessel. Ships bound both ways along the Gulf ports track mounted extra lookouts; they saw nothing.

Samkey, with her load of ballast and with her forty-three men, had vanished utterly and for all time.

Thus, darkly, Lawson was deprived of his first command. But less than a month later the company gave him another ship—the *Leicester*.

Leicester was the twin sister to *Samkey*; built in the same yards, to the identical design. The only difference was that she was younger by a year and that her *Sam* name had been changed to one that sounded more British. Launched late in 1944, she only served seven months in her original role as a war freighter. Demobilized, she lay fallow in a naval yard until she passed into the hands of the Federal Steam Navigation Company in June of 1947.

Now the loss of the *Samkey* had been no isolated incident. Of more than two hundred *Sam*-ships which joined the Allied merchant fleet during the war, less than half survived into the peace. Many of the missing ships died "normally" from torpedo wounds torn in their bellies. But a dismayingly large number of them did exactly what *Samkey* had done: they vanished, inexplicably and without a trace.

A quartermaster who sailed the convoy routes through the war years had this to say of those ill-omened ships:

"The Atlantic convoy job never was a cup of tea. What with the wolf packs and the mines and Heinkels, and the kind of weather the Western Ocean can brew up in winter, you expected to get clobbered any time. You might have called those the ordinary risks. But the *Sam*-ships were something special. They just used to slip away, usually in thick and heavy weather, and no one ever knew what happened to them. No wreckage. No survivors. No messages for help. Being torpedoed—it happened to me twice—was no ruddy joke, but at least you knew what hit you. The disappearing *Sams* now, they were something else. . . ."

Thus, even before the war ended, the *Sam*-ships had acquired a peculiar name amongst seamen: the Disappearing Sams. Seamen remember things for a long time.

Seamen hear things. When Lawson assumed command of *Leicester* at Gravesend in early February of 1948 there were few seamen aboard who did not know that, in 1946, a *Sam*-class vessel outbound from San Francisco for Taiwan had vanished without a trace. There were few who did not know that, in the early spring of 1947, another *Sam*-ship, under the Soviet flag and bound from Bombay to Chinese ports, had also sailed out of the sight of men forever. And there were none aboard who did not know of the *Samkey*.

Mysterious happenings at sea do not make pleasant matter for speculation amongst the men who live at sea. In this day and age when ships can radio each other, or the distant shores, with the ease of people talking in a narrow room, when ships can see each other with radar eyes over great distances, big ships do not pass into limbo with such abruptness that no man knows the manner of their passing. Yet, by February of 1948, at least fourteen *Sams* sailing in war paint, and three more sailing in peacetime rig, had disappeared without a single message from any one of them to tell the tale of how or why. Seamen remember things.

Under Lawson's command *Leicester* cleared from Gravesend for New Zealand in late February 1948, and worked her way westward with a full cargo under her hatches. She behaved very well all the way across the Atlantic, through the Panama and across the Pacific to her destination. Still, she carried with her a quality of unease. Lawson soon became aware of its presence—for an acute sensitivity to any unusual element in the little world that he commands is the mark of a good master. The missing *Samkey*'s name began to recur with increasing frequency in conversations both in the officers' saloon and in the forecastle. Her fate, and the mystery behind it, became a matter of engrossing interest to *Leicester*'s crew, who never forgot that *Leicester* was a *Sam*-ship too.

Leicester's people were not the only ones interested in the fate of the missing ship. During late June a handful of men met in the dusty confines of Admiralty Court in London to ponder the possible causes for the loss of *Samkey*. The investigators had little information on which to base conclusions, and the case might well have been adjourned without further light having been thrown on the *Samkey* mystery had not the Wreck Commissioner himself recollected an event which had taken place in 1943.

On January 2nd of that year, a merchantman bound from England for Canada suddenly developed a thirty-degree starboard list. Nothing her people could do helped to relieve the ship and she was forced to break convoy and to crawl precariously into St John's, Newfoundland.

Her name was *Sameveron*. She was in ballast at the time. And it was due to the shifting of her ballast that she had very nearly turned turtle and gone down.

The investigators pricked up their ears. "Where, and how," they asked, "was ballast carried aboard the *Sam*-class ships?"

The answer was startling. Ballast on *Sam*-ships—amounting to about 1500 tons if the ship carried no cargo—was not stowed in the deep holds at the bottom of the vessel but was carried *between the decks*, high above the empty lower holds!

The investigators immediately wished to know why the *Sam*-ships ballasted so high. There was no clear-cut answer. The best that a panel of experts could produce was a complex formula which seemed to indicate that *Sam*-ships became extraordinarily "stiff" and unhandy when carrying deep ballast; whereas ballasted 'tweendecks, they handled better.

"But," asked a member of the court, "would there not be a much greater risk of ballast shifting, in the 'tweendecks cargo spaces?"

The experts agreed that the risk was indeed greater, but they pointed out that, apart from the *Sameveron* case, there was no *certain* record of 'tweendecks ballast ever having shifted in any *Sam*-class ship.

Thus, the investigation ended on an inconclusive note:

Samkey had been lost through causes unknown. But there were those in attendance who were unusually thoughtful after the verdict. One of these was the Marine Superintendent for the Federal Steam Navigation Company.

When, on August 15th, two days after *Leicester* had again berthed at Gravesend at the conclusion of her New Zealand voyage, Captain Lawson once more sat in the office of the Marine Superintendent, he found himself thoroughly embroiled in the subject of ballast.

He heard, for the first time, the details of the official *Samkey* inquiry. He also learned that his next voyage with *Leicester* was to be from Tilbury to New York: in ballast.

"I've given the matter a good deal of thought," the Marine Superintendent told him, "and so have our naval architects and engineers. We've concluded that *Leicester* should be fitted with shifting boards."

In the great days of sail, shifting boards had been standard fittings on the grain clippers plying between Europe and Australia. They formed, in effect, a solid wooden fence running the length of every hold, along the ship's midline. They had originally been developed to prevent masses of loose grain from shifting to one side or other of the clippers when they lay over in heavy weather under a press of canvas. They had seldom been used since steam replaced sail, and the rule-of-thumb formula for determining their scantlings had long since been forgotten. But it seemed to the Marine Superintendent, and to Lawson too, that shifting boards, even of a makeshift nature, would materially reduce the risk of ballast shifting.

As soon as *Leicester*'s cargo was unloaded, the carpenters and shipwrights came aboard and went to work. Along the ship's midline, 'tweendecks, they erected a series of vertical steel stanchions—H beams—and welded the tops of each of these to the underside of the weather deck, and the bottom ends to the second deck. Between each set of stanchions they fitted horizontal planks of fir, three inches thick. Only when this work was completed did the ballast start to come aboard. Thames ballast it was; chosen because it did tend to settle firmly and so would resist the sliding impulse when a ship heeled over.

As the September sun streamed through the porthole, Hamish Lawson lowered himself into his desk chair, reached for his dispatch case, and took out a bundle of ship's papers. When he was quite ready, he rang the steward and told him to fetch the Mate.

First Officer James Bayley responded quickly to the Captain's summons and when he entered the cabin he found the old man deep in his papers.

"Well, Mister," Lawson said without looking up. "How goes the work?"

"Almost finished, sir. Another fifty tons in Number 3 and we'll be done. Fourteen hundred and ninety tons all told, and good stuff too. Just wet enough to settle firm. We've trimmed it level, all but Number 3, and that we'll finish before dark."

"You've kept a close eye on the stanchions and the shifting boards?" the Captain asked.

"Yes, sir. They're set up fine. We've brought the boards well up above the level of the ballast. There'll be no shifting of *this* lot."

The Captain turned toward his Mate and a slow smile softened his expression.

"Very good then, Mr. Bayley. You'd better take some leave ashore. We sail September 4th—at twelve o'clock."

CHAPTER 3

The hamlet of Nebek lies five hundred miles inland from Cape Verde on the west coast of Africa. It is an unprepossessing settlement of half a hundred souls in the heart of the Ulad Embarek sector of the Sahara Desert. It sees few visitors, but on September 1st, 1948, two sunburned Frenchmen—members of a government survey team— found themselves marooned there when the engine of their desert truck seized up.

The two men carried a portable transmitter, to keep in touch with their base camp, and they lost no time in sending off a radio message for assistance. The message sent, there was nothing for them to do except to huddle in a crematorium which masqueraded under the identity of a government rest-house, and pray for night to bring some relief from the searing sun.

Darkness brought little relief. The sun set in a barbaric burst of flame, and shortly afterwards thin clouds began to obscure the early stars. Out on the broken plains a wind began to rise. Gently at first, then with gathering strength, it blew through Nebek like the breath of a furnace.

One of the Frenchmen was a meteorologist, and even in this place of misery he had dutifully unpacked his instruments and set them up. An hour after dusk he went to take the readings. The temperature was 104 degrees Fahrenheit. Strangely, in this arid place, the humidity had begun to increase. But the barometer, which for days had been steady, had begun to drop.

The meteorologist noted the readings in his log, compared them with the morning readings, and whistled softly under his breath. The signs were clear.

Throughout the preceding week an immense area of high pressure—a roughly cylindrical mass of air five hundred or more miles in diameter—had been stationary over the southwestern desert, pressing down upon the sun-scoured lands below. Now the air within that invisible column, heated by an unbroken week of desert sunshine, had grown so hot that it had begun to rise. As it lifted, the pressure at ground level was decreasing. Already it had fallen below the pressure of the surrounding ocean of air so that atmospheric rivers had begun to flow in toward the base of the uprising column.

Returning to the rest-house, the meteorologist reported his findings to his companion.

"The high's become a low," he said. "Give it about twelve hours more and we'll be sitting in the middle of the damnedest sandstorm you ever saw."

But they were lucky. Toward dawn a relief truck came rumbling across the desert track, its lights hazy in the already dusty atmosphere. Before the sandstorm struck, the two Frenchmen were beyond its reach.

Throughout the next day a measureless flow of overhead air continued pouring into the base of the invisible column and streaming upward. It was a never-ending flow, for as the heated air reached great altitudes it spread out in all directions and slowly cooled, while at the column's foot the steady reduction of pressure resulted in an increasingly impetuous inflow.

Moving air is wind, and by midday on September 2nd the winds blowing through Nebek had reached speeds of fifty miles an hour. Sand and yellow dust were driving in a withering blast which forced men and animals to shelter.

All this went unremarked. The natives of the Ulad Embarek expected to experience such sandstorms every year about this time, and hardly thought more about them than about the daily rising of the sun.

They did not know that this intense disturbance of the atmosphere—which had now spread to cover an area some 700 miles in diameter—was in fact the genesis of a cyclone.

By September 3rd, the immense zone of inflowing winds began to accept the influence of the revolution of the earth and to begin a slow, circular pirouette: the incipient cyclone was ready to leave its desert womb.

On the morning of September 3rd, the weather station at Dakar on the Cape Verde peninsula recorded the presence of a major depression which seemed to be static over the West African coast, and was accompanied by strong if fitful winds. At 1200 hours, Greenwich Mean Time, Dakar Meteorological Station radioed its daily synopsis to Paris. At 1800 hours GMT Paris relayed the consolidated findings from all French reporting stations to all other nations which have an interest in the weather over the North Atlantic Ocean. By midnight, weather maps in twenty countries and on three continents were showing the development of a new low above Cape Verde.

Meteorologists in London, Washington, and a host of other cities studied the maps that night, and some of them made special note of the new low. It was not yet dangerous. It might never become dangerous. It might still dissipate its terrible potential and relapse into a local area of secondary storm. On the other hand, if circumstances were exactly right, it might begin to draw in upon itself, becoming infinitely more concentrated and powerful, and, if this happened, it might begin to march across the Western Ocean as a full-fledged hurricane.

At 0010 hours GMT on the morning of the 4th, the weather station on the Cape Verde Islands, 350 miles west of Dakar, reported winds of gale strength together with a sharp fall in the barometer. At 1200 hours this station reported a slight rise in pressure and a decrease in wind strength.

The die was cast. The hurricane would live. It had, in fact, already begun its westward passage—a passage which would follow a course four thousand miles in length, curving across the Western Ocean into the northwest.

PART TWO

CHAPTER 1

At 1200 hours GMT, September 4th, the Steamship *Leicester* recovered her anchors and cleared from Tilbury for New York; her destined course, some twenty-seven hundred miles in length, curving across the Western Ocean into the southwest.

Leicester had fine weather for her departure. As she made her way out of the Thames estuary and joined the stream of shipping in the Channel, the afternoon sun hung white in a shining sky. Smoke from the roaring fires beneath her boilers rose straight from the ship's stack and hung immobile while she drew away from under it.

Lawson was on the bridge, and with him was James Bayley. On deck the bosun and a crowd of sailors were completing the task of making the vessel shipshape for the open sea. Tarpaulins were being drawn over the hatches and iron bands were being clamped down around them and wedged home.

It was hot enough for Bayley to remove his uniform cap and mop his brow. He recollected himself part way through this operation, shoved his handkerchief back in his pocket and jammed his cap back on his head. It was easy to forget that the old man was a Navy Type. Bayley turned and caught the Captain's eye. There was a twinkle in it that brought a little colour to the Mate's wan cheeks.

"Good time ashore?" the Skipper asked, speaking apparently to the gyro compass.

Bayley cleared his throat and changed the subject.

"With weather like this, sir, we ought to make a record passage. Think it'll hold?"

"Maybe—and maybe not. The forecasts seem optimistic, but on this ocean God alone can tell what's going to happen next. We'd best take the bit of peace we're getting and be grateful for it."

During the first days of September, 1948, the North Atlantic was as close to peace as such a gigantic arena of conflicting forces can ever be.

Almost the whole of this oceanic world lay under the domination of the Azores High, a vast area of high barometric pressure centring above the outflung islands of the Azores and extending its sway over the entire central region of the North Atlantic. Across all its domains the Azores High brought settled weather. Summer still lay gently upon that mindless entity which most of us now call the North Atlantic, but which for a thousand years was known to mariners as the Western Ocean.

To some Olympian eye, or to some modern Puck encased in a metal capsule hurtling round the earth, that mighty oceanic plain would have appeared unmoving and at rest. But the Western Ocean never really rests, nor do its winds.

Spilling out from under the southern skirts of the Azores High, the warm and steady Northeast Trades blew over seas that once had been white-flecked with the sails of the great wind-ships bound down from European ports for South America and for Cape Horn. Only in the trough of the doldrums which separates the Northeast Trades from their companions of the Southern Hemisphere was the ocean quiescent. And even here there were forbidding signs of turmoil pending as an area of thickening cloud, swirling slowly out from the Cape Verde Islands, proclaimed the presence of a gathering disturbance.

To the northwest, along the American and Canadian coasts, an almost stationary continental high was giving birth to boisterous west winds. To the north, on the lip of the polar basin, late-summer storms were being born in the conflict between the cold Arctic air and the warm winds from the south.

So the winds still blew. Nor were the waters stilled. Landsmen sometimes think of ocean waters as being fixed in place, with only the surface being swept into motion by the winds. In point of fact, the whole Western Ocean is in constant flux. Some of the greatest rivers in the world flow through it and are a part of it. One of them, the Gulf

Stream, flows faster than the St. Lawrence; is sometimes five hundred miles in breadth; and runs between watery banks from the Caribbean to a point off Nova Scotia where it divides to send one portion of itself into the Arctic along the eastern shores of Greenland, and another across to Africa.

The ocean, seemingly at peace, is never at rest. Even the appearance of peace is something of an illusion, for within a few hours the collapse of a high pressure area, the onslaught of a low, or the birth of a cyclone can generate a furious conflict between wind and waters, which may engulf many thousands of square miles of ocean surface. There is no real peace upon the Western Ocean.

Bayley's prediction of a fast and peaceful passage had been, in reality, no more than a pious hope.

Nevertheless the weather held fine through the following five days and *Leicester* made good progress. Coming through the Channel she logged a steady eleven knots and by noon on the 5th she had passed the Lizard and was abeam of Land's End. Three hours later she took her departure from European waters, following the great circle course known to Atlantic navigators as Track C: for Ambrose Light and New York Harbour.

The card of the gyro compass repeater swung slowly as the vessel's head fell off, then steadied on 263 degrees. The Scilly Islands dropped astern and *Leicester's* bows began to rise and fall to the long roll of the broad ocean.

On the 6th of September Lawson personally inspected all the 'tweendeck holds, checked the trim of the ballast, and examined the visible portions of the shifting boards, together with their supporting stanchions. He noted that the ballast had set firmly—so firmly that his heels scarcely made an imprint on it. He also noted that the girders supporting the weather deck were badly in need of paint—and shortly after he emerged, a harried bosun was harrying a number of sailors down below with pots and brushes.

Lawson considered himself fortunate in that *Leicester* was a weather-reporting ship, her owners having volunteered her services in cooperation with the International

Meteorological Organization. She had been filled with a formidable array of instruments, and twice each day her operator dispatched reports to the nearest mainland radio station, receiving in return the general synopsis and the local forecast for the next few hours.

By noon on the 9th, *Leicester* had crossed the 30th meridian of longitude, midway between Newfoundland and Ireland, having been logging 240 to 260 sea-miles every day. She was behaving in exemplary fashion, carrying her ballast well, and handling like a lady. Lawson was pleased with her—but not so pleased as to be complacent. During the morning of this day, in response to a forecast of adverse weather ahead, he ordered the redistribution of water ballast in her double-bottom tanks, to see if he could improve her trim.

Toward evening on the 9th, the sky began to lower and the sea began to rise. By midnight the wind was blowing Force 6 from the west, a good strong breeze; and, as the night hours passed, both wind and sea increased to storm proportions.

Lawson did not sleep at all that night. He kept the bridge for eighteen hours. Every sense was straining to feel his ship, to assess her reactions to the storm. His orders to the helmsmen, or to the officer on watch, were issued with an unusual sharpness; and he was curt with anyone who spoke needlessly or who in any way distracted his attention.

Leicester rolled more than Lawson liked; but she came back quickly every time. It was a head sea she was encountering, and she took it well, shouldering the grey-beards aside easily enough. She was very lively; but that was only to be expected since even with 1500 tons of ballast she was a relatively light ship. Lawson did not force her. Long before the storm had reached its peak he had rung the engine room for reduced speed. She held her course at about six knots, and showed no inclination to misbehave.

The bosun, sent below on three occasions to check the ballast, reported that it showed no signs of shifting even during the heaviest rolls.

As the sun broke wanly through the thinning storm scud during the early afternoon of September 10th, its pale light gleaming over the grey waste of broken water, Lawson rubbed a hand over tired eyes, turned to the Third Officer whose watch it was, and said:

"I'm going to my cabin. Call me at once if anything un-unusual occurs."

The storm was passing and, for a time at any rate, the strain upon the Master of the *Leicester* was eased.

Lawson lay down, still fully dressed, and sleep came heavily and swiftly to him.

CHAPTER 2

The area of intense atmospheric disturbance which had appeared on September 4th over the Cape Verde Islands had, for five days past, remained unchanged—upon the weather maps. Which only meant that no new reports concerning it had been received. Having passed the Islands heading west, the disturbance would not encounter another weather-reporting station short of Bermuda—unless some ship happened to cross its path. Thus there was ample distance and ample time either for the disturbance to grow or to die away and vanish; with no man being any the wiser.

The incipient cyclone which had passed the Cape Verde Islands did not die away. During the five days while it remained unobserved by men, the immense mass of air, slowly swirling counter-clockwise around a centre of decreasing pressure, steadily gained momentum. As the speed of the forward movement increased, the circling winds blew with increasing violence and the whole gigantic system began to draw in upon itself; to concentrate its almost boundless latent energy into a coiling fury not much more than a hundred miles in diameter, which came more and more to justify the name: Cyclone—the Serpent's Coil.

The fact that the disturbance had remained unreported

for five days did not mean that it had been forgotten or was being ignored. The United States Weather Bureau, which had become one of the world's experts on hurricanes through long and tragic experience, was anxious to ascertain its fate. After five days without a report, the Weather Bureau decided to wait no longer. On September 8th, at 0800 hours, a long-range converted bomber of the United States Air Force took off from Guantanamo in Cuba and headed eastward, out to sea.

In 1948, hurricane hunting from the air was something new, fascinating, and extremely dangerous. Not much was known with certainty about the structure and inner nature of cyclonic storms, which in the Atlantic region are usually called hurricanes. It was known that the winds in the inner regions of the cyclone, close to the "eye," could reach momentary velocities of 250 miles an hour. It was known that the effective diameter of the Serpent's Coil varied from fifty miles to as much as four hundred and fifty. It was known that hurricanes required, on the average, five to seven days to reach their full magnitude, and travelled at a rate of from 10 to 30 miles an hour, usually along a parabolic course following a trough or general area of low pressure between adjacent highs. It was known that most North Atlantic hurricanes were born either over the Sahara and the Cape Verde region or over the western portion of the Caribbean Sea. So much—and not much more—was known to the crew of the reconnaissance aircraft which had been ordered up to locate and evaluate the vanished Cape Verde storm.

The aircraft climbed to 15,000 feet in clear and pleasant skies. Pilot and co-pilot could see nothing but amiable blue waters under them, an amiable blue sky above. The radar operator, his face glowing a putrescent green in the reflection of his scope, carefully watched the swing of the search beam; but there were no reflections, no pips to mar the glaring surface of the fluorescent tube.

The meteorologist too was watching his instruments, occasionally peering through the bubble dome at the distant horizon. The flight was smooth, routine and dull. There was only the heavy pulse of the four engines and the soporific glitter of the ocean far below to touch men's senses.

Five hours passed before the radar operator began to raise faint pips upon his screen.

"Got something coming up," he said over the intercom. "Looks like a heavy area of rain, bearing 103 degrees, range twenty miles."

"'Something' is right," the pilot replied. "Take a gander up ahead."

The sky was growing hazed beneath an immense canopy of cirrus cloud hanging at such an altitude that it seemed to be beyond the limits of the world. The sun looked sickly, paling into thin obscurity. Directly ahead of the aircraft a vast belt of purple twilight appeared to be rising from the sea. Streamers of altostratus cloud began to slip past above and below the plane, and gusts of rain swirled against the cockpit windows.

As the aircraft drove swiftly forward the surface of the ocean grew indistinct and, in a few more minutes, had darkened into invisibility. The plane began to buck and shudder as if to demonstrate its unwillingness to close with the purple wall which now loomed right across the eastern horizon, towering to a height of some 20,000 feet.

The pilot's voice sounded again in six sets of headphones.

"This is it. We're going down, to eight thousand and we'll go in at that level. Looks like a brute. Hang on, boys, here we go."

Ten minutes later the aircraft plunged into the Serpent's Coil.

For the next twenty minutes each man aboard the plane hung on to what was handiest—and hoped. Pilot and co-pilot, wrestling together with the controls, could barely keep the aircraft manageable. Time and again an unseen antagonist of wind drove her off balance, sent her slipping wildly down the dark and rolling sky, or threw her brutally upward into the blackness overhead. Her four engines roared almost unheard, their thunder overwhelmed by the voices of the wind. Lightning flickered steadily through crevices in the contorted clouds.

Sweat greased the two pilots' hands and ran down the hollows of their backs. The plane plunged on, its wings weaving until they seemed to be as flexible as sword blades.

Then suddenly the sun shone. There was no wind. And the aircraft was flying as steadily as it had done during the long inconsequential hours before it reached the storm.

Peering downward, the crew could see the shining sea; but when they looked about them, they were still surrounded on every side by impenetrable cloud. This was the centre of the coil.

The pilot, relaxing, swung the aircraft into a turn and for half an hour she cruised leisurely and peacefully within the calm heart of the hurricane while the meteorologist completed his work and the navigator checked the position by solar sights. The radar man—this was his first hurricane flight—stared fascinated at his scope, at the solid ring of pips that blended into a perfect circle around the position of the plane.

"It was like being in a glass barrel—right in the middle of it—and the barrel sunk in the darkest whirlpool of hell," he reported afterwards.

The aircraft had been steadily losing altitude and was now flying less than a thousand feet above the ocean. It was not an ocean which many men are privileged, or fated, ever to observe. It was white, not blue. The crewmen were appalled by the turmoil of those waters. They watched the monstrous waves rear up and explode into great geysers of foam. It was a sea gone mad—driven to terrible excesses by the wind and now, released from the wind's lash, leaping in a maniacal mood of self-destruction.

The aircraft began to climb again, still in the calm eye of the storm, and the radio operator started to transmit the meteorologist's report.

HURRICANE EYE ESTIMATED FIFTEEN MILES DIAMETER PRESSURE AT 1400 FEET 950.04 MILLIBARS POSITION 1345 HOURS

1750 NORTH 4700 WEST APPROXIMATE
COURSE 280 DEGREES SPEED 12 KNOTS
MAXIMUM WINDS FORWARD QUADRANT
130 PLUS

Climbing in brilliant sunshine, the plane began to
emerge above the hurricane at 16,000 feet; but still she
climbed. At 25,000 feet the crew, wearing their oxygen
masks now, could look down and see the hurricane spread
out below them. They could see the great vertical tunnel
they had just emerged from and, surrounding it, the gigantic whorl of wind-ripped cloud in a solid tangible dark
mass extending to the horizon on every side.

The co-pilot was given to homely similes. "You know,"
he said over the pilot's intercom, "it looks like a God-almighty big jukebox record. Imagine that. A record a
hundred miles across and three miles thick—playing a
piece nobody wants to hear."

The pilot did not answer. He was staring at the port
wing. From where he sat he could count at least fifty
missing rivets, and the wrinkles in the stressed skin of the
wing suggested that there were probably a lot more
missing in places he could not see. Very gingerly indeed he
swung the aircraft's nose around and laid his course for
home.

The report from the reconnaissance aircraft in flight was
received at Miami and put at once on a direct teletype
wire to the central offices of the United States Weather
Bureau in Washington. There three men were grouped,
intently watching the message coming off the machine.
One of them, the senior hurricane forecaster, tore the
completed message from the roll and walked with it to
an immense plastic-coated wall chart of the North Atlantic. Unhurriedly, but with sure strokes, he began trans-
lating the typed information into symbols, using a blue
grease pencil.

At the point where the aircraft had found the eye of the
cyclone he drew a cricle encompassing an area about 20
miles in diameter, and in the centre of it he marked a bold

letter L. Around this primary circle he drew six more concentric circles, each of which was an isobar representing an increase of atmospheric pressure: the last of them had a diameter of nearly 300 miles.

Finally he made a notation beside the letter L—vII/1400/8—thereby marking the position of, and giving an identity to, the seventh hurricane of the season, as of 2 P.M., September 8th.

The disturbance which had begun over the hamlet of Nebek nine days earlier had now become an entity, and a potential menace of such proportions that through the succeeding days it would engross the attention of several hundred meteorologists in weather stations spread from Venezuela to central Canada. Many men would match their wits and their technical skills against the Serpent's Coil in a concentrated effort to anticipate its action and, by the issuance of timely warnings to landsmen and seamen alike, to render its menace harmless.

But skill and wit are useless without information to work upon, and it was essential that the hurricane be kept under the closest observation. While it remained at sea, this observation could only be supplied by ships in its vicinity or by aircraft reconnaissance. But in 1948 a successful flight like the one made on September 8th might be followed by several days during which it was not possible to reach the hurricane. Shortage of proper planes, bad weather over landing fields, and mechanical difficulties could combine to deprive the forecasters of this invaluable aid—and this, in fact, was what occurred.

Two reconnaissance attempts on September 9th and 10th were failures; one when the aircraft lost an engine shortly after take-off, and the second when flying conditions became so bad that the aircraft was not even dispatched from its home field.

For two vital days the hurricane went its own way unobserved while the forecasters sweated out the hours.

It was not until mid-morning on September 11th that the ominous silence about Hurricane vII was broken. Then the teletype in the hurricane forecast room in Washington began to clatter, repeating the text of a message received

by San Juan Radio in Puerto Rico from the ss *Paladin* 800
miles southeast of Bermuda.

> SEPT 11 0900 AST POSITION 23.20 N 54.30 W
> HOVE TO DURING NIGHT HEAVY SEAS AND
> E AND SE WINDS FORCE 10 CAUSED DAM-
> AGE NOW PROCEEDING REDUCED SPEED
> WEATHER   MODERATING   WINDS   SSW
> FORCE 8 SIGNED MASTER PALADIN

The senior forecaster seized this message and began to
plot its information on the wall chart. When he had
finished he stood back and surveyed the results.

The original course of the hurricane had run from Cape
Verde almost due west to the position given by the aircraft on September 8th, but now it showed a pronounced
northwesterly swing.

The senior forecaster let his gaze project that course
along a continuing curve toward the waiting continent.

"It's speeding up, and turning north," he mused aloud.
"If it holds this course it might strike the coast near Cape
Hatteras and drive inland. But with the high pressure
area we've got sitting over the eastern seaboard, it's more
likely to keep swinging to the north and miss the land
entirely."

He turned back to his desk and spoke to his assistant.

"There's precious little to go on," he said. "But we'd
better issue an advisory warning anyway."

CHAPTER 3

September 11th broke clear. When Lawson came on *Leicester*'s bridge just before breakfast time, he found his
vessel pitching easily in the remnant seas of the previous
day's storm. A glance at the log showed him that she
had been making nine knots throughout the night, and a
pencilled cross on the chart put the ship only a hundred

miles east-southeast of Flemish Cap, and approaching the edge of the Grand Banks.

He nodded a good morning to the officer on watch, the Third Mate, and walked out on the starboard wing to smell the air and enjoy the failing breeze which still blew from the west. Then a thought struck him and he stepped back into the wheelhouse.

"If the wind shifts northerly," he said to the Third, "there'll be fog. Keep an eye peeled and let me know if the weather begins to thicken. The Banks are crowded this time of year and some of the fishermen don't bother overmuch with fog signals."

The Grand Banks, those submarine fish meadows which lie off Newfoundland, were crowded indeed. The radio operator, Sparkie, trying to work Cape Race that morning, had found it almost impossible to get clear air. The clutter of calls from the two hundred Portuguese, Spanish, Icelandic, Canadian and American draggers and trawlers was like an electronic babel. Nevertheless he had managed to hear the early morning weather schedule. The prediction was for continued clearing with light westerly to northwesterly winds and generally settled conditions.

Leicester ploughed on across the southern corner of the Banks. At about 1400 hours a grey-white wall on the western horizon came into view, and an hour later the world was blotted out by the prevading weight of a Grand Banks fog. *Leicester*'s deep-throated horn began to sound, gloomy and muffled under that almost tangible shroud. Moisture began to condense on all her upper works, dripping and thickening until it was running in cold rivulets down the sides of her houses and into the scuppers.

Leicester's isolation from the world seemed total—particularly to Sparkie who was now having trouble with his receiver, trouble he could not diagnose. He could no longer even hear the gossipy fishermen. Three times he checked the set thoroughly, without results, and there was a look of almost childlike perplexity on his youthful face as he contemplated the electronic enigma. There was no sense to it. He went out on the fog-sweating deck and checked the aerial leads, then he sat down at his desk and tried the key again. There was no answer from Cape Race —now less than 300 miles away to the northwest. He tapped out the call sign of an east-bound collier he had been talking with barely half an hour before. This time, after a long delay, he raised his man. The two operators chatted back and forth for a while and then Sparkie, hesitantly, explained his problem. He listened intently as the reply came rattling back.

> THINK NOTHING OF IT HEAVY FOG OFTEN REDUCES RADIATION AS MUCH AS HALF PROBABLY DUE DAMPNESS. YOU MAY ALSO HAVE DAMP SHORTING AERIAL INSULATORS. WILL CLEAR ITSELF WHEN FOG CLEARS. GO TAKE A NAP AND DREAM ABOUT YOUR GIRLS. REPEAT GIRLS . . .

Sparkie grinned and tapped out an appropriate reply. Then, there being nothing else for it, he signed himself off watch and curled up in his bunk with a magazine.

The day drew down, and the world contracted until *Leicester* was alone in her tiny hemisphere of fog.

Through the long night hours the ship ploughed on over slick and sombre seas. Her engines thudded gently like a heart at rest, and in the engine room Chief Engineer George Rhodes thought happily of his stamp collection and of the additions he would make when he prowled the stamp shops of New York.

The following morning Lawson laid off the vessel's course on the track chart and measured the remaining distance with his dividers. According to his calculations *Leicester* ought to have crossed the 50th meridian of longitude and to have come to the end of her great circle course by 0600 hours September 13th. From that point on she would steer a direct course for New York Harbour.

At 0930 hours on the 13th, the senior hurricane forecaster sat at his desk in Washington and stared moodily at the papers spread before him.

"How can we predict this lousy storm's course if nobody sends information in?" he asked querulously. "Yesterday the recce plane washed out again—today not a single ship reports from anywhere near the eye. We have to play guessing games."

"So we do," his assistant replied amiably. "And you're the top guesser around here. So where *is* our windy girl going today?"

"I wish I knew for sure. Anyway, she'll probably pass close enough to Bermuda to chase the tourists into the bomb shelters. Bermuda 'met' is standing by. They'll know, one way or the other, by ten tonight . . . can't we get *anything* out of those weather-reporting ships?"

"Sorry," the younger man replied. "There just isn't one in the vicinity. There's a couple of United Fruit boats too far south to help. And there's a Limey called the *Leechester* inbound on Track C, but he hasn't reported for forty-eight hours, and anyhow he's too far north to know what's going on."

The senior forecaster sighed, got up from his chair and went back to the wall chart. Tentatively he began extending the track of the hurricane from the last known position. As he did so, he consulted a slip of paper upon which he had written some cabalistic estimates of speed and direction interpolated from known data concerning the adjacent atmospheric conditions.

He was a long time making up his mind. Finally he drew a circle and marked the familiar *L* in its centre.

"That's where she *ought* to be at midnight," he said—but he did not speak with much conviction.

The circle, with its insignia of VII alongside, lay 80 miles northwest of Bermuda; and the predicted course from that point forward curved slowly away from the continent, heading toward the northern reaches of the Western Ocean.

Aboard the silent weather ship *"Leechester,"* at the same hour the hurricane forecaster was bemoaning the lack of information, Sparkie was staring at the mess of coils, resistors and tubes cluttering his desk He shook his head in complete bewilderment, and laboriously began for the third time to reassemble the dismantled set. Outside the porthole the sun was streaming down on a blue sea, and a flight of gulls skated through the air currents waiting for the cook to throw out the breakfast garbage.

The fog had passed, but its passing had not cured the recalcitrance of the radio: *Leicester* was still cut off from the world about her. Captain Lawson was beginning to show signs of impatience. He wanted to notify his company's agents in New York that he expected to arrive during the afternoon of September 17th. Agents require time to make their preparations, and they become less than amiable when a ship appears unexpectedly and complicates their lives.

"Well," Sparkie thought miserably, "they'll damn well have to be surprised." It was no fault of his that his set had been so mysteriously hexed. Maybe it was part of the general hex they said stuck to all the *Sam*-class boats. He picked up a soldering iron that had been burning a hole through a copy of Sherlock Holmes and, without much optimism, continued his task.

Leicester did not share his perturbation. As the day grew older, so did her big screw continue its unhurried beat, and the sea miles slid away beneath her keel.

While *Leicester* had been making her ponderous way toward New York, *Foundation Josephine* had been drydocked in Halifax. By September 11th she was ready to return to duty—spanking clean in a new coat of paint, and with all her gear in first-class order. On the morning of the 12th she sailed for North Sydney, there to relieve *Foundation Lillian;* she, in her turn, was due to go on dock at Halifax for her annual inspection and refit before returning to her permanent station at Bermuda.

Josephine made a fast passage north. Early on the morning of the 13th, she came abeam of the harbour entrance buoy at Sydney and shortly afterwards was easing into her berth at Kelley's Wharf, not far from where the *Lillian* was lying.

Half an hour after *Josephine* was moored her First Officer, a rotund and red-faced Newfoundlander named Wally Myalls, made his way up the dock to the office of the company's local agent. He was soon on the telephone to the Salvage Master, Featherstone, in Halifax, reporting his vessel's arrival and the fact that she was now on salvage station.

"Tell Captain Crowe," Featherstone instructed Myalls, "that *Lillian*'s due to go on dock for refit Thursday morning."

Foundation Lillian looked rather like *Josephine*'s twin sister, but scaled down considerably. For although *Lillian*'s tonnage and power were just half those of *Josephine*, both had the typical lines of the ocean-going salvage tug. Both sported the same paint scheme. Both had been built in war time.

Lillian was the product of United States yards and it

she lacked something of *Josephine*'s dashing lines, to her commander, Captain Crowe, she was still the sweetest vessel on the Western Ocean. He looked upon *Josephine* as a grossly overgrown travesty of what a tug should be. Every man to his own taste—and to his own command.

When Wally Myalls walked up *Lillian*'s gangway bearing the message from Featherstone, *Lillian*'s First Officer Jimmy Rose met him on deck. Rose was a massively built young Scotsman, with a burr as yet unmodified by the nasal twang indigenous to Nova Scotia.

"By heavens, Wally," Rose said solicitously, "you're getting fat as a swine. Must be easy living on that ocean liner of yours. Why don't you give up that kind of life and come to sea again in a real boat?"

Wally, who was slow-spoken and soft-voiced, grinned amiably.

"Yiss, Bye," he said. "But I'd as soon go to sea in a dory as *this* old bait-boat. Anyway it's you what has to go to sea. 'Feathers' was on the phone. You're due on the slip Thursday morning so they can patch this old tub up."

The two men, sturdy as the ships they walked, passed through the doorway into the accommodation, and in a little while the harbour air grew sweeter with the faint, elusive fragrance of red rum.

Shortly after the noon whistle in North Sydney sounded its shrill release from labour, *Lillian*'s radio operator appeared at the partly open door of Rose's cabin.

"Come on in, Sparkie," Rose called. "Come in and wet your nose."

Sparkie needed no second invitation. As he reached for the bottle with one hand, he stretched out the other hand to Rose, and in it was a message form. Rose glanced over it before handing it on to Myalls.

"Looks like *Lillian*'s going off duty just in time," he said. "Might be some work for you loafers for a change."

Slowly Myalls read the message, his lips forming the words in silence.

SYDNEY RADIO
1200 AST ALL SHIPS WESTERN APPROACHES

PART THREE

It was close on midnight, September 13th, and *Leicester* was about 200 miles southeast of Cape Race. The Second Officer glanced at the chart again and reviewed his calculations. In ten minutes, so he estimated, the ship would make her last alteration of course before raising Ambrose Light Ship. It was time to call the old man.

Lawson appeared on the bridge within minutes of receiving the call. From old habit he glanced first at the compass, checking the course, and then at the weather. The skies were magnificently clear and the quarter moon shone on a gently rolling sea.

"Has Sparkie got his box of tricks working yet?" he asked the Second. "It's about time he got us a little weather gen."

"No, sir," the Second answered. "He called me about an hour ago and said he thought he'd found the trouble but he wasn't sure. The glass has dropped a little in the last few hours, but nothing much."

Lawson made no response. He stepped into the chart room and carefully laid off the distance run, checking against the watch officer's figures. Lips pursed, he leaned over the chart a moment longer and then gave his order.

"Very well, Mister. You may alter now."

The Second called out the new course and the wheelsman, a diminutive cockney, repeated it with relish as he swung the wheel. "New York dead ahead," he thought. "Awaitin' there for me. Wonder if Sally still 'angs round the Greasy Spoon. By God, I 'opes she does."

Leicester's head swung slowly and smoothly onto the new course. Her movement through these calm waters was so easy that it would have been hard for a landlubber to realize that she was still at sea. The Second essayed an unasked-for comment.

"Often heard them call it the Big Pond, Captain," he said a little tentatively, "but this is the first time I ever saw it look like one in mid-September."

"Take a good look," Lawson replied. "Odds are you'll not see it like this again till summertime."

As if taking his own advice, he walked out on the port wing and took a long look himself. Then:

"Good night, Mister. I'm turning in," he said, and went below.

Lawson slept lightly, as most ship masters do. At 0700 hours on the morning of the 14th of September he came suddenly awake. For a moment he lay still, waiting until his conscious mind could identify the vague unease which had penetrated into his subconscious. *Leicester* was roll-ing—rolling heavily with a long, slow, ponderous motion.

Sunlight was streaming through the porthole over Law-son's bunk. As he began putting on his clothes, he glanced through the port and saw a shining morning. But of far more interest to him was the sea. Ten minutes later he was on the bridge, and in no pleasant temper.

"When did that swell begin?" he asked the watch of-ficer abruptly. "And why wasn't I called?"

The officer, a young and rather timid fellow who had only recently received his papers, stared in surprise at his unshaven captain.

"I can't say exactly when I first noticed it, sir," he said. "But it didn't begin to get really heavy till about half an hour back. And there was no sign of wind so I thought it wouldn't do to wake you up."

Remembering the youngster's inexperience Lawson re-pented of his abruptness.

"All right," he said. "But you don't need wind to give a warning, you know. That swell's running up out of the south'ard and whatever started it running must have amounted to a first-rate storm. Look at this." He stepped to the barometer screwed to the bulkhead and tapped it lightly.

"There's been a fall of two-tenths since midnight.

There's obviously a low ahead of us, or coming up from somewhere south, and at this time of the year that could mean something. You mustn't rely too much on radio and shore stations to tell you what the weather's going to do. You still have to be your own weather prophet when you sail deep sea.

"About that swell. Your textbooks should have told you that a swell like that can move at thirty or forty knots. Fast enough to put it well out in advance of the storm that caused it. If it's a tropical cyclone, then the cyclone itself may be five or six hundred miles away. It might not come anywhere near our course. Again, it might. I'm going for my breakfast now. Keep an eye on the southern sky. If it begins to haze over, let me know at once."

Somewhat stunned by this gratuitous lecture, the watch officer could only muster a delayed and almost whispered "Immediately, sir" at the retreating back of the old man. When the bridge was his again, he whistled softly under his breath and, with a sidelong look at the steersman, took Lecky's *Practical Navigation* off its shelf and began to thumb through it to the section on ocean swells.

Lawson had not gone immediately to breakfast, nor yet to his cabin for his morning shave. He had gone instead to the radio shack. He found his radio operator surrounded by an incredible litter of abtruse-looking gadgets. Sparks looked up as the Captain knocked and entered. He did not wait for the question to be asked.

"I think I have it, sir. Give me an hour, or at the most two, and I'll be back on the air."

Lawson nodded. "See that you get me an immediate weather report as soon as you can. I mean immediate." And with one last, rather wondering glance at the array of coils and tubes, he left the room and returned to his own cabin.

If Sparks had needed any incentive to spur him on, this was it. When the Captain himself comes looking for weather reports, then something's brewing. Sparks went back to his task with renewed energy. But despite his efforts it was not until mid-morning that he was able to receive a signal, and not until 100 hours that he was at last

able to contact Cape Race and ask for the current weather.
At 1105 he started for the bridge, almost at a sprint, with
a message in his hand.

Lawson took it from him and read it carefully.

GENERAL HURRICANE WARNING WEST-
ERN ATLANTIC HURRICANE PASSED FIFTY
MILES EAST BERMUDA 2230 HRS AST 13TH
ESTIMATED WIND SPEED AT CENTRE 140
MILES ESTIMATED TRACK SPEED 25 KNOTS
ESTIMATED LOCATION CENTRE 0800 HRS
AST 14TH 3730 NORTH 6400 WEST PRE-
DICTED COURSE NEXT EIGHT HOURS EAST
NORTHEAST PASSING 100 MILES EAST OF
SABLE ISLAND

Lawson strode into the chart room and in a few moments had plotted the position given for the centre of the
hurricane, and had roughed in its course. At 0800 hours
that morning the centre had lain about 500 miles away
from *Leicester*. At its predicted rate of progress, it was
probably now about 400 miles away from the ship's position, and roughly southwest of her. In about ten hours
time, if both ship and hurricane continued on their present
courses, their tracks would cross. The centre of the hurricane by then might be expected to be within twenty miles
of the point of intersection, approaching from the southwest, and in that case *Leicester* would be caught by it.

There was no way of knowing how large an area the
dangerous portion of the cyclone covered, but from past
experience Lawson knew that it would be uncomfortable
(to say the least) to be anywhere within a hundred miles
of the cyclone centre.

"Go see Sparks," he said to Bayley who had appeared
on the bridge as soon as the word of the approaching
hurricane reached him. "Tell him to try to work any other
ships which may be southwesterly of us. Tell him to get
the local weather from them. Have him try to raise Halifax, or one of the Yank shore stations, and ask for the
latest predictions on the centre's course and speed. Make

that a priority message. Have him explain that we're close to the predicted path. Too damned close for comfort—no, don't tell *him* that, that bit was meant for you. Come here and have a look. . . ."

It was a dismayed Sparkie who opened his shack door to Bayley a few minutes later. Even before Bayley could state the Captain's orders, Sparks was explaining that once more his set was out.

"I just don't understand it, Jim Everything was fine until five minutes ago. I could read both Cape Race and Sydney. Then they began to fade. I think I may be still getting a signal out, but I can't read a thing. I'll go back to work on it but I tell you frankly, I just can't think what's wrong."

When Bayley reported back to the bridge he half expected a tirade from Lawson. It was not forthcoming.

"He'll do his best," Lawson said. "It's not his fault, I'm sure. Meanwhile we'd better get on with it.

"We've three alternatives. We can change course to south'ard—which ought to keep us well to the east of trouble. We can stop where we are until either Sparkie gets the radio fixed or we're certain the hurricane's gone by between us and the shore. Or we can go about and steam back on our track.

"I don't think there's any real reason to try that last one. There's even less reason for the second—we'd just be a sitting duck if the thing should swerve farther out to sea. So we'll turn south and try to get behind the storm. We'll alter course at 1200 hours—that's in ten minutes' time. And none too soon maybe. Look at that sky."

Bayley, whose eyes had been on the chart, glanced up. To the southward the sky was growing hazy with high cirrus cloud which seemed to sweep the whole horizon from east to west. Lower down, toward a sea that was already growing leaden, there appeared to be a tenuous veil hanging above the surface of the water. It had no substance that the eye could find, yet it was there, illusory but real. The sun was gradually being encircled by a pale halo and its light was fading from white to dirty grey.

At 1200 hours the helmsman spun the big wheel down until the gyro compass lubberline stood at 180 degrees true—due south. *Leicester*, head-on now to the steadily increasing swells, began to lift heavily to their immense impetus. It was an uneasy motion—and it mirrored the feelings of the men aboard the ship. Without having any orders to do it, the bosun had undertaken to tour the holds and once more to check the ballast and the shifting boards. And in the forecastle the off-watch sailors got out their cards and glumly began a game of black jack. None of them voiced the doubts which all of them were feeling.

CHAPTER 2

By noon of September 14th the northwestern approaches to the continent were almost destitute of shipping. Many vessels which had put to sea from east coast ports on the 13th had turned back for harbour after receiving the hurricane warnings. Many others—including *Foundation Lillian*—had postponed their sailing dates. Most inbound ships from Europe had cut back their speed and were idling along, waiting for the hurricane to pass ahead of them—well ahead of them. But one of these inbound vessels, a German named the *Bodenhamer*, had been a little less cautious than the rest and had pushed westward a little too fast and a little too far.

At 1100 hours on the 14th, the *Bodenhamer* radioed Bermuda to the effect that she had been caught in the eastern fringes of the hurricane. She reported herself hove-to under the onslaught of winds of 100 miles per hour.

Bermuda radio relayed this report to Washington at once. Within minutes of its reception at the Weather Bureau, the hurricane forecasters were again clustered in front of the big wall chart. Quickly they plotted the new data, and then looked at one another anxiously.

Bodenhamer's position was almost one hundred and fifty miles east of the predicted track—and yet she was experiencing winds of a hundred miles an hour! The two facts were incompatible. No cyclone in history had ever contained such gigantic forces that its winds, at such a distance from its centre, would reach so great a velocity.

"Maybe the Kraut got his position wrong," said one of the weathermen hopefully. "Or maybe he scares easy and thinks a Force 8 gale is a real hurricane."

"And maybe not," said the senior forecaster. "Maybe *we're* wrong. We could be—easily. Look at the way the continental high is pushing out. It might be bringing enough pressure to bear on the cyclone's western flank to force it even farther to the east. Might be, and probably is. If only that Limey weather-reporting ship would show some sign of life. She must be somewhere close to the track by now. What was her name? *Leechester*, did you say? Have her called again. Meanwhile I think we'd better put a supplementary warning on the air."

> SEPTEMBER 14TH 1300 AST BROADCAST ON 500 KCY FROM ALL EASTERN SEABOARD RADIO STATIONS HANDLING MARINE TRAFIC
> ALL SHIPS WESTERN APPROACHES GENERAL HURRICANE WARNING ATLANTIC HURRICANE NOW BELIEVED CENTRED APPROXIMATELY 3800 NORTH 6300 WEST PREDICTED TRACK NOW SHIFTED TO THE EASTWARD CENTRE EXPECTED PASS 200 MILES SOUTHEAST CAPE RACE BY 1200 AST 15TH ALL SHIPS PROCEED ACCORDINGLY

Everywhere within range of the powerful shore stations ships' radio operators received this message and passed it on to their watch officers. These officers plotted the new information on their charts and prepared to "proceed accordingly" in order to remain out of the way of the circling monster of wind and water which bore the number Seven.

The *Leicester* was not one of those to hear this message.

DURING the early hours of the afternoon of the 14th the swell rolling up from southerly had become so heavy that Lawson decided to reduce speed a little. The ship's motion was still relatively easy, for the swells, though of gargantuan proportions, were wide-spaced and their slopes were gentle. They seemed to be moving beneath the ocean's skin, and the surface of the water remained smooth, oily, and unperturbed while monstrous pulsations ran rhythmically through the depths below.

There was not a breath of wind, even though the whole sky was now hazed by high cirrus cloud. The silence, and the tangible sensation which seamen feel when the atmospheric pressure begins to drop abruptly, combining with the eerie corpse light of the watery sky, gave rise to a general feeling of suspenseful waiting. Off-duty men moved aimlessly about the decks. Those who had work to do were grateful for it. Even the seabirds seemed affected, for the trailing stream of shearwaters, which had haunted the wake of the ship for many days, now began lifting high into the pale air and swinging away in cloudy flights toward the open sea.

On *Leicester*'s bridge, Cadet Officer Gardyne posted himself before the barometer and watched it with fascination. Slowly but implacably the needle was swinging to the left. It had read 30.8 inches the preceding noon. Now it hung on 30.3—a drop of half an inch in twenty-four hours.

Whatever Lawson's feelings of concern might have been, he gave no sign of them. Perhaps realizing that his continued presence on the bridge would only serve to accentuate the tension which was visibly developing, he returned to his cabin shortly after 1500 hours "to take a nap." But he did not sleep. Sitting in his armchair with an open book on his knees, he went over and over the limited information at his disposal concerning the approaching cyclone. Momentarily he hoped for a knock at his door and the entry of Sparks with the welcome news that the radio was back in operation. There was no knock.

Eventually he picked up his book and began to read. The words came clear to his mind, but he remained aware of the ship's every movement; testing, evaluating everything she did.

When Lawson returned to the bridge at 1630 hours, he found Bayley on watch. The barometer had fallen slightly but not alarmingly. However the sky *had* become alarming. To the south a great swelling arch of black and forbidding clouds was beginning to rise from the horizon. Lawson recognized it at first glance, and the anticipation of approaching trial grew sharp in his mind.

"Hurricane bar, Mr Bayley," he said.

Bayley nodded.

"Yes, sir. It began to look like a 'bar' a few moments ago. I was about to call you."

Lawson watched the ominous black arch for a quarter of an hour, and even during this short interval it seemed to grow, humping up from the horizon, spreading east and west. Above it, and around the hemisphere of sky, the high clouds were thickening, growing more opaque. A light, aimless breeze that seemed to come erratically from every point of the compass had begun to play about the ship. Lawson noticed that there were no gulls or other seabirds anywhere in sight.

He stepped into the chart room and looked at the pencil marks which showed his ship's position and the predicted path of the hurricane.

"Bayley," he said, as he came out into the wheelhouse once more. "I don't like the look of this. I think the cyclone must be veering sharply easterly. We'll do the same. Alter course three points."

As *Leicester's* bow came round, her motion changed. Down in the stokehold and engine room men glanced at one another with unspoken questions in their eyes. Chief Engineer George Rhodes turned to his Third Engineer and spoke in his ear.

"We've altered to the east. The old man must think we're too close to the blow for comfort. Get around now and see how things stand. Warn the oilers to watch themselves—and watch the machinery. We want no breakdowns. I'm going to the bridge for half a moment."

By the time Rhodes reached the bridge, the appearance of the sky had changed again. Now the whole south horizon had gone black with distant clouds which were so dense they seemed as palpable as rock. The breeze had become wind, blowing gustily through the ship's rigging, and it had steadied out of the northeast.

Lawson greeted his Chief Engineer with a slight smile.

"Felt like some fresh air, George? Looks like we'll get a lot of that before the night is over. How are things down below?"

Rhodes turned away from the barometer.

"Never better. We had some trouble with a bearing in one of the auxiliaries this morning, but it's been replaced. You think that thing is going to smack us?" He pointed the stem of his pipe at the rising bar of the still distant cyclone.

"Probably," Lawson said. "We ought to be east of the worst of it, but we're still going to have some weather. You'd better count on that, and batten down."

It was unnecessary advice, and both men knew it. Rhodes had been at sea for twenty years and knew his business. All the same, he did not linger on the bridge. When there was trouble brewing, he liked to be where his gaze could run over the glistening reaches of his own domain of brass and oil and steam.

In the galley the cook was sweating over supper. One of the mates had told him to hurry it along, and he was hurrying for all his worth. He had no taste for trying to prepare meals during a heavy blow.

On deck the bosun and the Second Mate were busy with two gangs of deckhands. Every lashing was being checked. The Chief Officer had already inspected all the hatch covers and had taken his flashlight and gone below for one last examination of the innocuous-looking world of ballast. As the ship rose and fell with the long slow passage of the swells, he could not see so much as a trickle of displaced sand, or a handful of pebbles brought to life by the vessel's motion.

Leicester's people wasted no time about their evening meal. They bolted their food and returned to their varied tasks. Whatever the outcome of this night might be, they and their ship would be ready for it.

At 1930 hours the hurricane bar, by then arched across almost the whole southern sky, was being obscured by low cloud driving rapidly from east to west. The barometer had begun to fall much more steeply and the wind had risen to Force 4, from east-northeast. The smooth surface of the sea was being fretted by waves which rose sharply and ran away across the line of the great swells. At 1945 hours Lawson had the helmsman alter to 94 degrees—almost due east. The ship had turned her back upon New York.

In his radio shack, Sparkie laboured over his set with the energy of desperation. Although he did not know in detail what was taking place, he guessed that the radio failure had brought the ship into what might turn out to be a very uncomfortable position. He felt obscurely that this was all his doing. For the twentieth time he ran through the manual of emergency repairs seeking some clue to the hidden fault.

Then at 2000 hours, and with an appalling suddenness, the world went dark. Heavy storm clouds rolled in over *Leicester* and the pale light of the sky was obliterated. Wind came with the cloud, and in a quarter of an hour it had risen to a strength of Force 7 from due east. The waves had ceased to be mere children of the sea and were maturing at a frightening rate, lifting more and more sharply, and growing whitecaps on their crests. Through the murk ahead, ghastly reflections of hidden lightning could be faintly seen.

On the bridge Lawson spoke to his Chief Officer.

"We're for it, Bayley. I'd guess we're already in the

right front quadrant, and we're going to go well into it. How did that ballast look?"

"Steady as a rock, sir."

"Keep the wind fine on her starboard bow," Lawson said. "It'll be shifting southerly as the centre of the hurricane moves up. Don't drive her, but keep her moving the best you can."

At 2100 hours Bayley, who had remained on watch despite the fact that the Third Officer had come up at eight bells to relieve him, made an entry in the log.

> *Weather deteriorating rapidly. Barometer 30.1 and still falling steeply. Wind* ESE *Force 9 to 10. Steep head sea and heavy southerly swells. Heavy rain reducing visibility to three hundred yards. Vessel rolling and pitching heavily and taking some solid water across the foredeck. Speed reduced to 40 revolutions, making good about 5 knots on a course of 44 degrees. Ship steering badly.*

At 2120 the bridge phone rang. Bayley answered it.

"Sparks here. I think I'm getting out now, but I still can't receive except on the emergency set, and there's nothing close enough for me to reach. I'm still working on it though and—"

Bayley cut in. "All right," he said curtly. "There's probably damn little to hear that can do us any good now. But let us know at once if you pick up anything."

"Sparks can transmit," he told Lawson as he hung up. "There's something, anyway."

Lawson did not comment. He was standing beside the helmsman, staring alternately at wheelhouse windows, which were now a shimmering obscurity as the hard-driven rain flowed over them, and at the face of the compass. The card was swinging erratically and the helmsman was sweating as he wrestled with the wheel.

Bayley moved over beside Lawson and glanced at the card. Even as he did so, *Leicester* began to fall off the wind. She swung through an arc of almost three points before the helmsman could check her and start her slowly back toward her course. Lawson's face was grim.

"Hold her up, man, hold her up!" he said harshly.

This was no more than a reflex. The helmsman was obviously doing all he could. Despite his efforts, *Leicester* was becoming more and more unmanageable.

Lawson picked up the phone and called the engine room.

"That you, Chief? She's getting very hard to handle. Reduce your speed ten revolutions."

By 2230 the sounds of the storm were making it difficult to hear the human voice, even within the confines of the wheelhouse. The anemometer mounted on the exposed flying bridge was being driven so fiercely that its cups were no more than a blur of motion. The windspeed dial in the wheelhouse was showing sustained velocities of 90 miles an hour, gusting occasionally to 95. When Lawson cautiously opened the door leading to the port wing of the bridge, the back eddies from the thundering river of the wind nearly tore it from his hands. He fought his way out on the wing in an effort to assess the state of the surrounding sea.

Rain lashed into his face with the strength of driven shot. His hastily donned slicker whipped against his body. Shielding his face with one hand, he gripped a stanchion with the other and peered out into the roaring night. It was almost impossible to distinguish sea from air. The storm waves now rose to fearful heights but, as they lifted, so were their tops blown clean away—blown away in great streaks of foaming scud which mingled with the almost horizontal blasts of rain.

Lawson was breathless and streaming wet when, a few moments later, he struggled back into the wheelhouse. Bayley beckoned to him to look at the barometer. It had fallen two-tenths of an inch during the past two hours.

Leicester was now well into the right front quadrant of the cyclone. As the centre drew closer, the maelstrom of revolving wind steadily changed direction, coming ever more southerly. The helmsman fought to keep the furious wind just on the starboard bow, but the wind was

veering far more rapidly than the towering seas could
alter the direction of their march; as a result, the ship
was often broadside to their assault. Her motion was becoming wilder and wilder. Shuddering and creaking, she
rolled, pitched and yawed at one and the same time. In
her accommodations, men clung to whatever was at hand
—clung and held on. There was no question of moving
about outside—the decks were being continuously swept
as great seas boarded her and churned themselves to
foam against her hatch coamings and deck gear.

Even with two men at the wheel, she could no longer
be held even remotely close to her prescribed course. By
2300 hours she was virtually out of control, and at 2305
Lawson ordered a radio message to be transmitted.

STEAMER   LEICESTER   POSITION   4220
NORTH 5800 WEST IN FULL HURRICANE
HAVING DIFFICULTY STEERING ALL SHIPS
KEEP CLEAR ALL SHIPS KEEP CLEAR

The message was repeated over and over again on
Sparkie's chattering key; but there was no assurance that
it would be heard. The ship's receiver still sat mute and
useless in its iron cage.

In any event, it was not much more than a gesture Lawson was making, for if there had been another vessel in
the vicinity, neither ship could have detected the other's
presence in that blind world of wind and water until
collision had become unavoidable.

Down in the engine room, Chief Rhodes clung with one
arm to a polished stanchion at the control station and
watched his Third Engineer hanging on to the big brass
throttle wheel. When *Leicester* began her plunge, as each
new abyss yawned before her, Rhodes raised his free
hand and held it poised. He waited until the bow had
sunk well past the horizontal, then dropped his hand in
a compelling gesture. Instantly the Third began to spin
the wheel, cutting off steam to the labouring pistons. The
mighty shaft began to slow until the propeller, now lifting
high out of the rolling waters, was barely turning. Again

Rhodes' hand went up and, as the ship lethargically began to lift her head, he signalled the Third to give the engine steam.

Rhodes knew the strain that a propeller alternately labouring deep beneath the surface and then racing wildly above the water could place upon the shaft. And he knew only too well that a broken shaft might easily doom the ship and all within her as the vessel became totally helpless under the mauling of the hurricane.

To the men deep in the bowels of the ship, her motion seemed less extreme than it did to those on the bridge or to the seamen clustered about the mess table and hanging on to it with tight-gripped hands. All the same, *Leicester* was throwing herself about in a terrifying way. As she rolled over to port, Rhodes glanced at the clinometer. It showed that she was heeling to 32 degrees. He watched it with a cold concentration until the hanging indicator began to swing gradually back towards the vertical.

"Much more of that," he thought to himself, "and she'll go over on her beam ends." For he, like every man aboard the vessel, was thinking of the 1500 tons of ballast stowed 'tweendecks, high up above the surface of the tortured sea.

At midnight the watch officer again filled in the log.

> 2400 *hours. Full hurricane. Wind* wsw *gusting to* 110 *m.p.h. Barometer* 29.8 *Zero visibility. Mountainous broken sea. Ship taking heavy solid water fore and aft, rolling to* 30 *degrees. Barely maintaining steerageway at* 30 *revolutions. Vessel answering helm only with extreme difficulty. Position probably abeam the hurricane centre and very close to it.*

Fifteen minutes later the needle of the windspeed indicator fell swiftly back to register a mere 40 miles an hour. The barometer stood fairly steady at 29.8. But the motion of the seas surrounding the vessel seemed suddenly to become wilder and more savage. Observation of these things confirmed Lawson's suspicion that the eye of the storm was abeam of his ship and close at hand for, as the wind dropped toward the calm centre, the untrammelled seas could be expected to leap skyward in a paroxysm of tortured water.

He turned to Bayley and shouted in his ear:

"I think we'll pass just outside the eye. The wind should come south any minute now. Stand by to get her headed round—"

The last part of his instructions was drowned out as a towering column of black water leapt high above the wheelhouse and came crashing down upon it with a jar which shook the entire vessel.

Both men were still looking at each other in mute astonishment when a second wave of even more immense proportions struck *Leicester* a pile-driver blow upon her starboard flank.

The ship heeled down as if she never meant to stop. Men clung to each other or to anything at hand. The clinometer in the engine room swung to 35, 38, 40 degrees and hung there for a dreadful minute. From somewhere under Lawson's feet there came a prolonged and heavy rumbling as of a muffled avalanche—it was a sound more felt than heard. It ceased at last and then, with mind-destroying sloth, *Leicester* began to roll slowly back. Slowly, slowly, until the clinometer showed 30 degrees port list . . . and there it stayed.

Clawing his way up the canted deck of the wheelhouse, Lawson reached the phone and rang the engine room. There was no reply, and from the dull silence in the ear-piece he knew it was out of order. He dropped it and motioned to the two helmsmen who were clinging to the wheel, their feet skidding out from under them. The little cockney caught the motion and managed to crawl crab-wise to the Captain's side.

Lawson yelled in his ear.

"Get below! Tell the Chief ballast has shifted. Tell him to transfer the oil from the port tanks to the starboard tanks."

Nodding his head, the sailor scrambled for the companionway and vanished, helping himself along with his hands like a wounded monkey.

Now Lawson took stock of the position. His ship was almost lying on her side in the cockpit of a hurricane, but she was still under way, and still answering, if in an erratic manner, to her helm. The calm centre of the cyclone was apparently going to miss her, and she was probably even then entering the right quadrant, with the prospect of being clear of the worst of the wind and sea within four or five hours. If she could be kept from broaching to and rolling completely over, if the list could be reduced, by judicious transfer of oil fuel to the high starboard side—then she might yet be saved.

Twenty minutes after she took her list, Lawson made his way out on the port wing of the bridge to try to see for himself how things looked on deck. He was standing on the wing when, without warning, a monstrous sea loomed up astern and engulfed the entire vessel in one foaming cataract.

The swirling waters swept around Lawson, broke his hold on the railing and carried him, struggling futilely, back into the sea. Half-drowned and wholly deafened by the thunder of the cataclysm, he thrashed his way to the surface just as a second mighty sea rose, lifted him, and carried him back aboard the stricken ship. When the water drained away, Lawson found himself jammed against the railing of the boat deck, thirty feet aft of the bridge wing from which he had been swept away.

He had no time to appreciate the miracle of his deliverance. Even as he struggled to his feet, he saw that his ship had been cruelly, and perhaps mortally, bludgeoned by the blows of those two great seas. He could not get his footing on her deck at all, and he realized that her list had now become so extreme that she was practically on her beam ends.

As soon as the Chief Engineer had received the message about the ballast tanks, he had started the fuel pumps working in order to transfer oil from Number 3 port deeptank to Number 3 starboard. The pumps had just begun their attempt to restore the ship to something nearer an

even keel when she was struck by the sea that carried
Lawson overboard.

She went over farther than any man could have believed a ship could go—and live. She went far beyond the
range of the clinometer. When she eventually came back,
she steadied with a 50-degree port list. Her terrible roll
to port had been accompanied by a heavy trembling
throughout the ship, and this time every man aboard
knew instantly what it meant. The remaining shifting
boards had given way and the rest of the 1500 tons of
ballast had gone sliding over to the port side.

It was then 0040 hours on the morning of September
15th. *Leicester* was almost totally helpless. She still had
steam, but though her propeller churned the angry seas
she could not be manoeuvred. Within a few minutes she
had swung broadside and her lee rail was completely
under water. At times she rolled down to 70 degrees,
dipping her boat deck well below the surface of the foam-
white sea. So steep was the angle of her decks that men
could not walk upon them at all; instead, they crawled
or slithered in the angles between the bulkheads and the
floors. The cold green waters roared up against her,
poured through open accommodation doors and ports on
the port side, and ran down into the engine room. Most
of her people felt that only minutes would intervene
before she turned turtle and went down.

Bayley was still in the wheelhouse when Lawson—Bayley had seen him leave the wing door and then vanish
overboard—reappeared like a saturated ghost via the
companion from the after accommodations.

Grasping the edge of the chart table, Lawson heaved
himself erect. "Sound the emergency signal!" he yelled.

In that frightful confusion of darkness and near-despair,
the signal was sounded, but perhaps improperly—or, at
any rate, some of those who heard it seem to have inter-
preted it improperly as the order to abandon ship.

Sparks, two of the engineer officers, and a handful of
oilers and seamen crawled out onto the boat deck and
ripped off the canvas cover of Number 4 boat. Sparks and
the Third then climbed aboard while someone knocked

off the gripes which locked the boat in her chocks, so that she was held in place only by rope lashings and by the falls to the davits.

At 0115 hours Lawson ordered Bayley to go aft and cut the falls on all the boats, so that they would have a chance to float free in the event the ship capsized.

Bayley inched his way along the boat deck, being very nearly swept overboard by a sea which broke right to the base of the funnel. On reaching Number 4 boat, he took out his knife and began sawing at the falls. In that rain-lashed darkness he could see nothing more than a few inches from his nose, nor could he hear anything above the howling of the wind, which was again building up in strength as the immediate centre of the cyclone drew away from *Leicester*.

As he hacked at the last of the sodden ropes, Bayley thought he heard a faint voice shouting, and thought he caught the one word "gripes." But in that instant another great wave thundered aboard, swept over the boat deck and, as it boiled back into the sea, it took both port boats with it. Spun end for end, they disappeared in the flying spume.

Clinging to the chocks with both hands, Bayley was still coughing water out of his lungs when a half-heard scream close to him made him turn his head. Lightning flashed suddenly in the blackness of the sky and by its flare he saw the body of Able Seaman Whittaker come hurtling down the canted deck, crash into the bulwarks, and vanish into the sea.

Bayley realized that to cut loose the two starboard boats would only guarantee their loss, and so he now began the slow crawl back toward the shelter of the bridge.

When the ringing of the emergency bells pierced the sounding fug of the engine room, Rhodes immediately ordered his oilers, firemen and other hands on deck. Accompanied by the Second Engineer, Rhodes himself chose to stay below, though there was nothing that he could now do for the doomed ship. The pumps could no longer continue with their task of transferring fuel and water to the starboard tanks, and in any case the vessel's list was now so severe that even the successful transfer would have done little if any good.

Alone in that echoing vault, watching the gleaming shaft turn under the grip of the three great pistons, Rhodes and his Second waited further orders. Through the companion hatch above them a steady stream of cold salt water poured into the engine room and ran along toward the stokehold. There was a danger that this water would reach and quench the fires. But there was a much greater hazard present—one that stiffened the muscles in Rhodes' neck. Because of the list the ship was carrying, the pumps, recirculating fresh water from the condensers to the boilers, were already sucking air; and, if the boilers did not get sufficient water, there would be an explosion which would make an abrupt end to *Leicester's* slim chances of survival.

Shortly before 0200 hours, Bayley returned to the bridge where he reported to Lawson that Sparkie and the Third Officer both appeared to be missing. These two, with Whittaker, meant three men gone.

With her helm lashed down (no human hands could have held it now), *Leicester* was still under way, and making three or four knots—but aimlessly and in the trough of the waves. Lawson desperately wished to keep her under power, but when he was informed of the danger of a boiler explosion he had no choice but to order the Chief to cut off the oil-feed to the fires. A seaman carried the order to the head of the engine-room companionway where Rhodes and his Second Engineer had finally retreated.

Rhodes elected to go below himself to shut off the feed. At the same time, he had some hopes that he could start one of the auxiliary pumps and, by forcing oil overside, protect the ship from being continually swept by the onrushing waves. Hanging like an acrobat to the iron ladders, he reached the feed valves and closed them; but as he attempted to reach the pump he slipped on the oily gratings and crashed down upon them with such force that he tore a six-inch gash in his scalp Unconscious, he rolled against the stanchions where he hung precariously above the still pulsating machinery.

Ten minutes later, when Rhodes had not returned, the Second Engineer climbed down to look for him, followed by the Fifth and by a fireman. Together these three managed to heave Rhodes back on desk and wedge his body securely betweeen a hatch coaming and a stowed cargo boom on the starboard side.

The driving spray and rain soon brought Rhodes round. Still dazed, he struggled to his knees only to be pitched down the full width of the deck into the lee scuppers, where he again struck his head and was again knocked unconscious.

By the grace of God he had been seen, and two seamen risked their lives to slide down after him and haul him into the accommodations bare seconds before *Leicester* put her rail ten feet under a surging sea.

The ship's carpenter was not so lucky. Caught on the open deck by the full force of a sea breaking over the bows, he was thrown down to the lee side with such force that his body was smashed like a ripe pumpkin against the bulwarks. For a few minutes his limp corpse was washed back and forth in the scuppers, then it too vanished.

There was little now that *Leicester*'s men could do to save themselves or their ship. Many of the survivors huddled in the saloon or in the starboard alleyways, for the most part in pitch darkness for, as the steam pressure fell, the generators slowed and died. The deck officers, crowded together on the bridge, clung to whatever they could find. . . . And all men waited.

Only in the confines of the radio shack was there anything to do. Here the Fourth Officer, assisted by Cadet Gardyne, tried doggedly to get the emergency transmitter into operation to send an s o s. Neither one was a radio expert, but this did not dismay them. Time and again they checked the equipment, followed the leads, checked the battery power source, and then laboriously tapped out their s o s. They had no way of knowing if it was being read; but considering that all the aerials had been either swept overboard or torn from their insulators, they did not have much hope.

Still *Leicester* lived. No man knew how, or why.

Lifting soggily to the great seas, she slithered off their crests, fell heavily into the troughs, took solid water up her deck until it reached the centre of the hatches, then somehow shook herself free and slowly lifted back to life again.

Forty-three men, knowing that death might come at any instant, waited the hours out.

By 0400 hours there was a notable easing of the seas and wind. According to Lawson's calculations, the centre of the hurricane must then have been 80 or 90 miles away to the northward. He began to believe that his ship might still survive until help came. She might even, if it proved possible to raise steam, remain afloat into calm seas where something might be done to reduce her list. Lawson broached this idea to the Second Engineer who immediately volunteered to go down into the engine room to see what he could do.

It was a useless journey. The Second returned in half an hour, covered with fuel oil, to announce that there was now four feet of water over the gratings of the engine-room floor, and that the fire boxes were completely flooded. Without steam to run the pumps, the water could not be removed. Without fire, there could be no steam to run the pumps.

By 0700 hours, the dawn which few aboard the *Leicester* had ever again hoped to see broke grey over a dark and tormented sea. The Serpent's Coil had passed, leaving in its wake the confused turmoil of mighty waves breaking under the tattered flags of driven clouds in a high sky.

By all the rules, *Leicester* should have taken her long plunge hours before. But in the dawn hours of September 15th she still remained afloat.

PART FOUR

CHAPTER 1

SEPT 15 0800 AST ALL SHIPS NORTHWEST APPROACHES AND GRAND BANKS ATLANTIC HURRICANE CENTRED APPROXIMATELY 4330 NORTH 5330 WEST PREDICTED TRACK NORTHEAST PASSING 100 MILES SOUTH CAPE RACE INTENSITY RAPIDLY DECREASING TO STORM STRENGTH MAXIMUM WINDS 70 MPH SMALL CRAFT SHOULD CONTINUE TO TAKE PRECAUTIONS

Time was running out for Hurricane VII. The Great Wind had struck its ultimate blow. It had run its terrible course across four thousand miles of ocean in ten days; but within the next twenty-four hours the Serpent's Coil would begin to disintegrate. Where the hurricane had been, there would remain only a diffused area of stormy weather spreading out into the lonely northern reaches of the Western Ocean.

The morning weather report made welcome reading aboard the scores of vessels which had been inbound for North American ports, only to find their ways blocked by the threat of the approaching hurricane. Some of these vessels—those closest to the path—had been forced to heave to and wait. Others, farther at sea, had simply reduced their speed. Still others had altered course to pass behind the hurricane. The eventual result of all these manoeuvres had been to produce what was literally a deep-sea traffic jam, particularly at the western terminus of the populous Track C.

The Captain of the U.S. Liberty *Cecil N. Bean,* inbound from Bermuda from British ports, was fully alive to the fact that this portion of the ocean had become uncomfortably overcrowded. According to his radio operator, there were at least thirty-seven other ships within fifty miles of him at dawn on September 15th—and this in an area where fog might at any moment initiate a gigantic game of blindman's bluff.

Having been assured by the morning weather report that it was safe to proceed once more, the Master of the *Cecil N. Bean* decided to abandon Track C entirely and to steer a continuation of his own great circle course direct for Hamilton, Bermuda, and so avoid further propinquity with the covey of ships assembled all around him.

Bean's deviation from the normal track was voluntary, but the passage of the hurricane had forced a good many other ships to an involuntary change. One of these, the Argentinian Steamship *Tropero*, bound for Montreal from Buenos Aires, had been chivvied three hundred miles eastward of her intended track. By the morning of September 15th, *Tropero* was quite alone and sailing in a portion of the North Atlantic which very rarely saw a vessel's smoke.

She was carrying a full cargo of frozen meat—and her refrigeration system was of dubious reliability. Consequently, once he had received the message that the hurricane was now well to the northward of him, *Tropero's* Master lost no time in laying a direct course for the entrance to the Gulf of St Lawrence.

News that the hurricane was well clear of the shipping lanes was gratefully received by the scores of ships which had delayed their departures from New England and Canadian ports. By mid-morning ships were streaming out of some major ports in such numbers that it was reminiscent of the great wartime convoy departures.

North Sydney, being a minor port, did not present an equivalent spectacle of maritime bustle—but at least one ship was preparing to put to sea. She was the *Foundation Lillian,* now twenty-four hours overdue for her appointment in Halifax.

The world of shipping on the western approaches to the continent was almost back to normal before noon of the 15th.

The scene which met the eyes of the surviving members of *Leicester*'s crew, as the dawn light strengthened, was one of almost total despair. The seas were still running twenty feet high—enough to swamp any lifeboat which tried to brave them. In any case, both *Leicester*'s port lifeboats had vanished, and her two starboard boats looked to be impossible of launching. The ship, while retaining a permanent list of 50 degrees, was rolling so far beyond this angle that seas were breaking at the feet of her derrick masts. It would have been a herculean task to swing the starboard boats out far enough to clear the great sweep of canted hull.

The only way to move about the ship at all was to crawl. There was no surface level enough for a man to stand upon. Bulkheads, walls, and floors were all so steeply angled that they offered no purchase for a man's feet. There was no power, and no heat, aboard the ship —and therefore no hot food. And the temperature had dropped to less than 45 degrees.

Leicester's people could not leave their ship—and they dared not remain with her. With each slow roll, it seemed inevitable that she must continue all the way over. Every time she hesitated and rolled painfully back again, men's thumping hearts ran wild within their breasts.

There was little they could do to occupy their hands or minds. The Fourth Officer and Cadet Gardyne continued their almost hopeless task of trying to get the ship's emergency radio into operation, though they knew by now that they were not getting a signal out.

A fireman named Hudson climbed into one of the starboard boats and assembled the crank-operated emergency transmitter carried there. For seven hours he turned that crank, and for seven hours his tiny short-range transmitter sputtered its prearranged distress signal into empty air.

Twice the Second Engineer dared the descent into the engine room, but there was nothing to be done in that cold cavern where the water splashed across the gratings amongst the dead machines.

Bayley and the bosun prepared both starboard boats so that these might have a chance of floating if, or when, the ship capsized. Then they tried to move along the lee alleyway to close the ports and accommodation doors through which the sea was finding its way to the engine room. But each time they hazarded the passage the vessel rolled down to her boat deck and threatened to drown them if they ventured into the alleyway.

Some of the men dragged mattresses out of the rooms and spread them in the angles between walls and floors, and there they tried to rest. But who could rest, knowing that every roll the big ship took might be her last?

On the bridge, Lawson wedged himself behind the chart table while he tried to determine the vessel's position by dead reckoning. He knew she was already well off any normal steamer track. The Gulf current and a steady northerly breeze were setting her toward the southeast. Lawson realized that if the ship was not soon seen, or if she failed to draw attention to herself by radio, she would enter a no-man's land of water where few ships ever ventured.

Overhead the sky was clearing under the noon sun. The wind freshened, and off the port bow a sharp fin cut the surface of a wave. A lone gull appeared from nowhere and began circling the dying ship, screaming as if in shocked surprise at the fantastic spectacle.

CHAPTER 3

Captain Cowley of *Foundation Josephine* and Captain Crowe of *Foundation Lillian* sat together in the agent's office. It was a sunny September morning and seen through the window North Sydney harbour had the crisp clear look about it that comes with a brisk northwest wind from off the land. Crowe had just returned from the shipping office, having cleared *Lillian* for Halifax. In half an hour his ship was due to sail.

"That's the first hurricane I ever knew to come this way that brought no business for you fellows," the agent was saying.

Cowley grinned.

"I don't mind being left in peace occasionally. This is the first time I've lain undisturbed in harbour through a really bad blow since I joined Foundation Company."

Crowe lifted his glass, took a long swallow, and said:

"It's the weather boys that did it. For once they got their predictions right. Any ship that got into trouble this time would have had to be a proper Jonah boat. . . . Well, boys, I'm off to Halifax."

Crowe drained the glass, stared hopefully into its empty bottom for a moment, then got to his feet, shook hands, and started for the door.

"Cowley—you better watch that man," he said, pointing to the agent. "He cuts his rum." And he was gone.

At 1100 hours on September 15th, a deckhand cast off *Lillian*'s lines. Slowly she backed into the stream, swung about on her heel and headed down the harbour. By noon she had cleared the land and was feeling the heavy swells, the legacy of the vanished hurricane, beneath her keel. Crowe altered course to clear Flint Island, then went below for lunch. He looked forward to reaching home port and seeing his vessel into the hands of the fitters and shipwrights. It had been a long time since she or he had had a holiday; and they both deserved a good one, he felt.

Captain Crowe finished his meal and took his leisurely way back to *Lillian*'s bridge. The weather was fine and clear, with a stiff breeze blowing. Six or seven miles away, off the starboard quarter, he could see Cape Breton. Long before dawn *Lillian* would be safely moored in Halifax and he would be free to pack his grip and go ashore.

He was still dwelling on this idyllic prospect when Sparkie mooched onto the bridge and, without comment, thrust into the Captain's hand a message which he had just decoded. Sparkie's normally pleasant face was as dour as that of a teetotalling Wesleyan in a distillery.

HALIFAX RADIO FOUNDATION LILLIAN
FROM FOUNDATION MARITIME
PROCEED ASSISTANCE PORTUGUESE
TRAWLER GASPAR DISABLED BY HURRI-
CANE 4450 NORTH 4840 WEST SS BIBBS
STANDING BY BUT UNABLE TO TOW CASU-
ALTY

There was a long silence on *Lillian*'s bridge; a deep and pregnant silence. But three minutes later Crowe gave a new course to the helmsman and *Lillian* swung and steadied on 097 degrees, bound for the troubled *Gaspar* 500 miles away to the eastward.

CHAPTER 4

Aboard *Leicester*, the day did not progress—it crawled across the universe of time at an infinitesimal pace. Every man was now on deck, wrapped in whatever clothes he had been able to lay his hands on. No one cared to go below into the accommodations, not even to recover his most personal belongings. They clustered on the starboard side of the boat deck where the afternoon sun brought a little warmth—and where they were near the two remaining boats.

More to keep them occupied than because he believed it would prove of any real use, Lawson decided that all hands should turn to and make some rafts. The men assembled under the eyes of the bosun and the deck officers and did what they could to obey the order. There was not much to work with. Empty barrels were lashed together and some spare hatch boards were found with which to deck these makeshift floats. At 1400 hours one of them was launched on the end of a slack line, as a test of its seaworthiness. It did not get far. The first sea that struck it tore the lashings asunder and sent barrels and planks skittering away in all directions. Interest in raft making subsided after that.

There was really nothing to do but wait. Wait for what? Wait in the faint hope (and it grew fainter by the hour as *Leicester* drifted into the southeast) that another ship might appear on the horizon. Or wait for the moment when the ship would give up her apparent defiance of the laws of equilibrium and finally capsize.

At 1830 hours a heavy wave struck the starboard side. The ship rolled to port, then gave a sickening lurch and for an interminable minute failed to make any attempt to come up again. Each man aboard her thought, "This is it." They were wrong. She did come back—dreadfully slowly, but she came.

It was enough for Lawson.

"We can't wait any longer, Bayley," he said. "We've got to try and launch those starboard boats. The sea's gone down a bit and they should live, if we can only get them clear of the hull without staving them in or capsizing them. Anyway, we've got to try."

It was a heart-breaking, hopeless task. When Number 1 boat was swung outboard and the falls were eased, she immediately crashed into the canted hull and smashed her gunwales. It was too dangerous to attempt to lower her with anyone aboard; but without several men to hold her off from the hull she refused to go at all. After an hour's agonizing struggle, they managed to drop her part way down the forty-foot steel cliff; there she caught on the projecting ledge of the bilge keel and turned over, spilling her gear into the sea.

Everyone aboard recognized the futility of what they were doing, but they had nothing else to do—and at any moment *Leicester* might take another of those horrifying lurches, one she would not recover from. So they worked on, cursing, sweating and sometimes bleeding, while the darkness gathered.

As the light faded, a vanguard of grey clouds began to sweep across the sky above the ship. There was weather coming. The northwest wind had been freshening for several hours and already there was a formidable chop running counter to the still fearsome seas left by the hurricane.

The men who were still fumbling, almost blindly now, with the starboard boats, had become resigned to death. They were convinced that if another storm should break there would be no more need to hope. The darkness deepened and the rising wind whined in the torn rigging.

It was 2100 hours. The little cockney seaman had somehow made his way down into the galley, lighting his way with matches, in order to scrounge biscuits and cans of meat to feed his comrades. As he emerged from the starboard alleyway and was about to swing himself up the ladder to the boat deck he turned and took a long look in the direction of England and of home. And then he yelled.

"Lights! There's lights out there!"

Instantly every head turned toward him, and every eye followed the direction of his pointing arm.

Out on the remote black sea a glimmering white light showed steady as a star. It was the masthead light of an oncoming ship.

Within minutes, Lawson and Bayley had broken out the flares and rockets, and soon the sky above *Leicester* was livid with their glare.

The faces of the men clutching the starboard rail flamed crimson and they looked like denizens of hell. But in their eyes was hope.

Aboard the *Cecil N. Bean* the officer on watch stared almost with awe at the pyrotechnic spectacle that had exploded out of the darkened sea.

"It looked," he said afterwards, "like a Fourth of July in Washington! Those fellows sure weren't taking any chances on being missed!"

Answering rockets were fired from the *Bean* even as she altered course.

An hour later she was lying to, within a quarter of a mile of the wreck. Because of the increasing rough sea and the mounting wind her Master dared not come any closer. To have done so would have meant needlessly endangering his own ship. He planned to launch two lifeboats to windward of the *Leicester* and, as they bore down on her with wind and sea astern of them, he intended to manoeuvre the *Bean* to leeward to be ready to pick the boats up again when they had taken off *Leicester*'s people.

It was not to be that easy. Ten-thousand-ton ships are not designed to handle like yachts, particularly in half a gale of wind with a heavy cross-sea running. The *Bean* had trouble enough coming broadside to the wind in order to launch her boats at all; and she had trouble with the boats themselves. The first one got safely away, but the second was so badly damaged when a sea slammed it against the mother ship that it had to be hoisted back aboard. *Bean*'s master did not care to risk his two remaining boats unless it was absolutely vital—he had his own crew to think about, and he was still a long way from Bermuda.

The boat that did get away made heavy weather of the trip. Those watching her progress with the aid of a searchlight from the *Bean*'s bridge frequently lost sight of her completely as she dropped into the troughs of the heaving seas.

When the boat eventually reached *Leicester* and tried to come around on the lee side, a breaking sea buffeted her so sharply that the rudder lifted from its pintles and was carried away, leaving the lifeboat almost unmanageable.

She was then within fifty yards of *Leicester* and her coxswain cupped his hands and bawled out an appeal for a spare rudder. Able Seaman Mair immediately slipped the rudder out of the pintles of one of *Leicester*'s remaining boats; then, tying a lifeline around his waist, he plunged into the breaking seas and swam with the rudder to the *Bean*'s boat.

Although she was again under control, the lifeboat could not make a landing on the *Leicester*. The big ship was rolling so heavily that any attempt to have done so must inevitably have proved fatal. Lawson thereupon told his men to jump for it and he himself helped them down the sharply sloping deck.

Ten men made it, and then the *Bean*'s boat pulled away. The state of the seas was such that she could not risk taking any more.

In the meantime a second vessel had arrived upon the scene. This was the *Tropero*, whose people had also seen the *Leicester*'s rockets. *Tropero* immediately launched two boats and these bore down upon the crippled ship.

By this time the storm had reached maturity. In the darkness of the night, blinded by scud and flying spray, rescued and rescuers alike fought for survival. Not all of them were successful.

By midnight the *Bean*'s boat had taken so much damage that it too had to be hoisted back aboard. However, one of *Tropero*'s boats still kept the seas, although it dared not approach within several hundred feet of the heaving hulk of *Leicester* around which the surf curled and boiled as if she been a reef awash.

Nearly half of the *Leicester*'s crew were still aboard her. Now, one by one, they threw themselves into the churning sea. Some of them struck out for *Tropero*'s boat but could not find it in the confused and angry darkness, and so turned instead toward the brightly lighted *Bean* which lay almost a mile away to leeward. Some made it to the *Tropero*'s boat and were hauled into it.

By 0200 hours on the morning of the 16th of September, Captain Lawson was alone upon the deck of his vessel. Tying the waterproof packet containing the ship's papers to his waist with a lanyard, he said his private farewell to his first merchant command. Then he jumped.

Half an hour later *Tropero*'s boat reached him, and took him aboard.

The donkeyman greaser and the Chief Steward were never found. In retrospect the survivors remembered a shark which had appeared during the morning of the 15th.

At 0345 hours the searchlight of the *Cecil N. Bean* was switched off, and in that instant the abandoned vessel vanished from men's sight. The two rescue ships resumed their respective courses and their navigation lights grew faint and disappeared over the black horizons of the night.

PART FIVE

CHAPTER 1

Big, jut-jawed and pale-eyed, Robert Featherstone sat in his fusty office in Foundation Maritime's dockside building on Water Street, Halifax. One heavy hand was drumming upon the surface of a scarred desk, the other waved a half-smoked cigar in the blue air to emphasize a point. "All right," he said. "The Coast Guard thinks she's gone. Her Master thinks she's gone. The skippers of those other two ships think she's sunk. *But I don't think she has!*"

This last was a bellow that shook the thin partitions of the room.

The gentlemanly company executive held his ground. He was, if not used to the Salvage Master, at least somewhat inured to him.

"Look, Cap," he said placatingly. "You're probably right, and everybody else is probably dead wrong, but you know it costs two thousand dollars every day *Josephine's* at sea. She might be out there a week and never find so much as a floating barrel. What do we tell head office in Montreal if *that* should happen?"

The big man thrust his cigar forward as if it were the head of a harpoon.

"Don't tell them a bloody thing!" he said. "None of their business. What do *they* know about the sea? *I* tell you that boat is still afloat. And if we get her—an abandoned ship, mind you—we'll have a million dollars on a string!"

Captain Robert Featherstone—"Cap" to his face, "Feter" on radiograms, and "Feathers" behind his back, but *never* "Bob"!—was a man born to the sea, bred by the sea, and gifted with a capacity for self-certainty which, to ordinary men, sometimes seemed to smack of egomania. He believed in himself and trusted himself as few men dare to do. And he acted, always, out of that belief and trust. If he ever felt a serious doubt about his own infallibility, no man who had worked with him during his thirty years in the deep-sea rescue and salvage business knew about it.

Featherstone was a subjective man. His decisions were seldom, if ever, predicated on neatly correlated facts of the slide-rule variety. He did things because he "knew" they were the right things to do—even if, as was often the case, he could not explain why or how he knew. He trusted his physical senses implicitly, and he gave unquestioning allegiance to those flashes of intuitive perception which modern men often denigrate as hunches. A simple man, perhaps. Yet through thirty years of salvage work during which he had been responsible for the rescue of some hundred and fifty vessels from the seas, reefs and rocks of the Atlantic coasts, he had found sufficient reasons to believe in his own abilities, sufficient reason to follow those intangible promptings of the inner mind for which no logical support can be advanced.

The executive sighed.

"Okay, Cap," he said. "We'll play it the way you say."

This little contretemps, now effectively ended, had had its beginnings at 0920 hours September 16th, when the Canadian Armed Forces' Air/Sea Rescue Headquarters at Halifax had called Foundation to pass on an intercepted radio message.

SS TROPERO CALL SIGN LOKS TO NEW YORK COASTGUARD 0800 16 4027 N 5510 W ABANDONED BRITISH FREIGHTER LEICESTER FROM LONDON TWO PARTLY SUBMERGED LIFEBOATS—MASTER TROPERO

To this rather inscrutable message, the officer on duty at Air/Sea Rescue had been able to add the information that a ship called the *Cecil N. Bean* had reported picking up survivors at this position, but had not confirmed what ship they had come from.

The moment the call from Air/Sea Rescue was completed, Featherstone telephoned the Company's agent in North Sydney.

"Get hold of Cowley. Tell him to sail at once, 4027 North 5510 West. An abandoned ship. 4027-5510. Got it?"

Only then did he rise from his chair to check the location of the abandoned vessel on the wall chart. Only then did he inform the senior officials at Foundation Maritime that *Josephine* had been dispatched 450 miles to sea on information which, besides being extremely vague, would seem to indicate that the ship to be rescued was sinking fast, if indeed she had not already gone down.

Recalling the incident long afterwards, Featherstone could and would give no reason for his instantaneous conviction that the *Leicester* was still afloat. He simply felt that she had not yet sunk. He also knew that every minute counted if there was to be any chance of saving her.

"Deep-sea salvage is a gamble from start to finish," he has said. "You don't have time to stop and weigh the odds. You have to move, and move damned fast, else the weather may sink the ship or someone else may put a line on her.

"Usually we work under the Lloyd's Open Form contract, which says right on it: 'No Cure—No Pay.' The master of the casualty, which is what we call a ship in trouble, signs it and so does the master of the tug. Unless the tug gets the casualty safe to port, we don't collect a red cent for the job. No cure—no pay. But if we get the casualty to port, we get paid proportionate to the risk involved.

"In *Leicester*'s case, she was abandoned so there couldn't even be a Lloyd's Form contract. She wasn't ownerless, you understand. When her crew left her she became the property of the underwriters who had insured her, and who would have to pay the shipping company if she became a total loss. The fact that she'd been abandoned made it seem pretty likely she was going to be a total loss, and so nobody, not even the underwriters, was interested in paying us to go out looking for her. We had to go 'on spec' or not at all. If we never found her we stood to lose a lot of money—running ocean tugs comes high. If we found her we still had to get her into a safe port, and if she sank somewhere along the way we wouldn't get a dollar for the work we'd done and the risks to our ships, our gear and our men. The odds were stacked against us. On the other hand, if we got her into port we could make a salvage claim equal to at least half her current value; and we'd be pretty sure to get it.

"*Leicester* was strictly an 'on spec' job, and if we were going to stand a chance of bringing it off we had to send *Josie* to sea as fast as possible. If we'd sat around on our rumps waiting till we got confirmation that *Leicester* was still afloat, she mightn't have been by the time we got there. Or maybe somebody else would've got there first. I didn't figure to waste any time."

Cowley wasted no time either. He received Featherstone's message at 1015 and by 1038 *Foundation Josephine* was under way. One of her oilers, who had been quietly killing the fag end of a bottle in the company of a lady chum in an hotel room five blocks away, managed to rejoin his ship in time. But only just. As he came pounding down the dock, he was seen to be wearing nothing but a bath towel clutched insecurely around his midriff with one hand—in the other hand he carried his shoes. Salvage men do not stand upon the order of their going when they hear the recall signal from their vessel's siren.

Once *Foundation Josephine* had her orders, Featherstone turned to the task of getting more information about the casualty. Cables were dispatched to Lloyd's in London—that clearing house for news of maritime disasters. Air/Sea Rescue was asked to monitor all radio calls from sea; and a telephone call was placed to the United States Coast Guard Headquarters in New York.

None of these produced immediate results but at 1100 hours the U.S. Coast Guard relayed the following message:

SS CECIL N. BEAN TO USCG NY
SS LEICESTER ADRIFT WITH BAD LIST DUE
SAND BALLAST SHIFTING EXPECT HER
CAPSIZE MOMENTARILY LIFEBOATS AND

RAFTS ALSO ADRIFT ONE MAN HAS HEAD
INJURY PROCEEDING BERMUDA—MASTER

This was followed half an hour later by a second radio-
gram.

RESCUED 20 SURVIVORS LEICESTER RE-
MAINDER CREW 18 TAKEN ABOARD AR-
GENTINE STEAMER TROPERO ADVISED BY
MASTER LEICESTER SIX OF CREW LOST
DURING HURRICANE AND VESSEL NOW
COMPLETELY ABANDONED—JD MASTER
CECIL N. BEAN

Neither of these messages gave much comfort to
Featherstone. Obviously the *Cecil Bean*'s Captain did not
share the Salvage Master's optimism as to *Leicester*'s
chances of remaining afloat. Nor was Featherstone's
"hunch" given much support by the reply to a query he
had sent from Halifax Radio to the *Tropero*. This he received at 1330 hours, by which time *Josephine* was already at sea, logging sixteen knots.

FOUNDATION HALIFAX YOUR QUERY LEI-
CESTER LISTED 70 DEGREES SINKING
CONDITION WHEN DEPARTED MONTREAL
—CAPTAIN TROPERO

And a little later that afternoon a notice to Mariners
issued to all ships by the U.S. Coast Guard seemed to set
the seal on *Leicester*'s fate.

ABANDONED VESSEL LEICESTER LAST RE-
PORTED 4027 NORTH 5510 WEST LISTING 70
DEGREES IF STILL AFLOAT CONSIDER SE-
VERE MENACE TO NAVIGATION

First Mate Jimmy Rose leaned against *Lillian*'s gyro compass standard and stared morosely out to sea. As Halifax

drew farther away to the westward, *Lillian*'s people were feeling distinctly glum. The tug badly needed an overhaul and a refit, even as her people badly needed a few weeks ashore; but this excursion in search of a disabled Portuguese trawler promised to delay both refit and shore leave by at least a week.

Rose was still on watch when Sparkie joined him.

"Good medicine," said Sparkie. "Here, read this."

"This" was a scrawled copy of a message—abrupt and to the point.

TRAWLER GASPAR SANK CREW RESCUED
SORRY—MASTER BIBBS

"Sorry?" said Rose, a great smile beginning to break across his face. "I'd buy that man a drink, if he was here."

"Two drinks," said Sparkie. "Maybe three."

Lillian was a much happier ship when, ten minutes later, she spun about on her heel and headed for Halifax. Captain Crowe gave Sparks a message for dispatch to Featherstone announcing the fate of the unfortunate *Gaspar* and reporting that *Lillian* was now hightailing it for home.

Featherstone received this message at 1445 hours. At 1505 Sparkie again appeared on *Lillian*'s bridge. This time he said nothing at all but thrust a message into Rose's hand with a gesture which implied that it was probably poisonous.

BRIT SS LEICESTER ABANDONED 4027 N
5510 W STOP PROCEED AND WORK WITH
JOSEPHINE WHO IS PROCEEDING FROM
SYDNEY STOP KEEP CONTACT WITH JOSIE
STOP ACK—FETER

In a way it is too bad that Rose's immediate acknowledgement could not have been transmitted exactly as he uttered it; but there are certain standards of decorum which must be observed on the international air waves.

Five minutes later *Lillian* altered to the south.

From the log of the *Foundation Josephine*:

> 1312 *Scatari Island abeam. Altered course South 3 degrees East. Wind East by South Force 2. Fine and clear* . . .

Leaving the land behind her, *Josephine* shoved her bows through the heaving substance of the seas. Her broad low stern seemed to settle deeper into the water as her big wheel thrust her forward at sixteen knots upon her search.

For John Cowley, on her bridge, this search promised to be no easy matter. He had a position for the *Leicester* but that position was based upon the dead reckoning of yet another ship and it might well be in error by many miles. And Cowley was aware of the unpredictable effect of the Gulf Stream and its subsidiary currents, which would be setting the derelict—if she was still afloat—rapidly off to the eastward, while whatever local winds she might be encountering would introduce yet another and totally unknown factor of drift.

The Atlantic is a big ocean. A ship is a small thing on its expanse. Consequently it was with considerable relief that Cowley received a message from Featherstone late in the afternoon to the effect that *Lillian* was joining in the search.

From the north and from the northwest two tugs were now converging on an unmarked point of ocean.

At dawn on the 17th both tugs were bucketing into heavy seas that were growing steadily rougher under the lash of a Force 7 gale that had sprung up out of the southeast. Neither tug reduced her speed, but aboard both of them men felt an increase of tension as they wondered what the gale would do to a ship which lay abandoned with a list of 70 degrees.

At 1000 hours Robbie Vatcher, *Josephine*'s radio operator, called the bridge.

"I've just raised the *Tropero*. She's heading for Montreal and pretty near abeam of us, about fifty miles to the northeast. You want to talk to her?"

Cowley did. And *Tropero* had some useful information

to impart. She reported that *Leicester* had been drifting south-southeast at between four and five knots when last seen. That had been thirty hours ago. If the drift had remained constant, she might by this time have drifted up to 140 miles from her last-reported position. Cowley plotted the probable new position, altered course toward it, and notified *Lillian* of the change. He also suggested a rendezvous and Crowe agreed to meet him at the intersection of two lines of latitude and longitude at 2200 hours.

At 1800 hours *Lillian* was pounding through very rough seas in the vicinity where *Leicester* had been abandoned. The lookouts were doubled, and at ten minutes past the hour one of them spotted something. *Lillian* swung off course to close—but the object was only a floating timber.

By 2200 hours visibility was almost zero—night and the storm between them had sealed off the world. But darkness means nothing to the eyes of radar. At 2212 Wally Myalls, watching the scope on *Josephine's* bridge, picked up a blip to the northward. He watched it closely for ten minutes and tentatively identified it as the *Lillian*. Using the radio-telephone on the wheelhouse bulkhead he was soon talking direct to Crowe. An hour later the two ships were driving side by side into the southern darkness.

Throughout that night, *Josephine's* radar screen was never left untended. (*Lillian* had then no operative radar.) When one officer's eyes began to tire, he was relieved. All night the two tugs ran along the track which *Leicester* might have followed in her drift; but nothing showed upon the radar scope.

At midnight Cowley dispatched a general message under *Josephine's* call letters: MFML.

ALL SHIPS KEEP SHARP LOOKOUT FOR ABANDONED BRITISH FREIGHTER LEICESTER PRESUMED POSITION 3947 NORTH 5443 WEST AT 1200 GMT 16TH STOP ANY INFORMATION CONCERNING THIS DERELICT SHOULD BE PASSED TO MFML.

No ships replied.

At 0200 on the 18th, Cowley called Crowe on the radio-telephone and the two captains arranged to make a co-ordinated search beginning at daylight. *Josephine* was to search south, then west, while *Lillian* was to proceed south, then east—both vessels following rectangular search patterns.

Dawn brought a worsening of the weather.

From *Josephine's* log:

> 0600 *Wind* NE *gale force Vessel rolling and pitching heavily. Speed reduced. Motor boat cradle smashed and washed overboard by heavy sea. Port rubbing band torn apart drawing several bolts causing leaking in forward mess deck . . .*

Both little ships were being pounded, and pounded severely. *Lillian,* forced to reduce to seven knots, was taking solid water green across her bows, and only rarely could the helmsman see anything through the streaming wheelhouse windows. A lookout, posted on the railed enclosure atop the wheelhouse called Monkeys' Island, was forced to rope himself to the binnacle standard, and the binoculars with which he was supposed to sweep the tilting horizon had become so saturated as to be completely useless.

At 0946 hours Cowley dispatched a message to Halifax:

> SEARCHED 3120 SQUARE MILES LAST NIGHT WITH RADAR STOP NO LUCK STOP CASUALTY REPORTED 70 DEGREE LIST WHEN LAST SEEN STOP MAY HAVE SUNK IN ROUGH SEA STOP HUGE SWELL NOW PREVAILING STOP LILLIAN AND JOSEPHINE NOW MAKING COMBINED SEARCH TO SOUTH AND EAST STOP REQUEST AIR SEA RESCUE DISPATCH AIRCRAFT AID SEARCH

In Foundation Maritime's offices at Halifax, the mood was pessimistic—except in Featherstone's den. Every in-

dication seemed to point to the certainty that *Leicester*
had gone down, but still Featherstone refused to allow
reason to submerge the intuitive faculty which had so
often served him well. Although little had been said
about it, he was aware of the mounting pressures on him
to call off the search.

Grimly he picked up the phone and spoke to the Com-
manding Officer at Air/Sea Rescue Headquarters. He
got small comfort there. The officer had neither the inclination nor the authority to risk one of his planes and
crews searching for an abandoned ship which had most
probably gone down long since. Had *Leicester's* people
still been unaccounted for, the response would have been
different. As things stood, the answer to Featherstone's
request was an unequivocal refusal.

The search at sea continued. But *Josephine* and *Lillian*
were now no longer the only salvage vessels interested in
Leicester.

About 200 miles out from Bermuda, a spanking big
ocean-going tug belonging to the Dutch firm of L. Smit
& Company was making her leisurely way westward toward the port of Hamilton, there to take a damaged ship
in tow for delivery to New York. The *Zwarte Zee* was
one of a large fleet of powerful tugs which Smit used for
towing "dead" ships and such unpowered objects as floating drydocks, dredges and big barges, to all parts of the
oceanic world. Contract towing was the mainstay of Smit's
business—but none of his tugs ever turned down a chance
at a deep-sea salvage job.

Throughout the afternoon, *Zwarte Zee's* Master pon-
dered over a sheaf of messages relating to the *Leicester*.
He had at his disposal all the information which had been
passed to Foundation from external sources. But he had
none of the information transmitted between the two
Foundation tugs at sea or between them and their base in
Halifax. Many years earlier Foundation Maritime had
contrived a complex code in order to frustrate the attempts
of rival tugs to take advantage of privately acquired
knowledge; and on the *Leicester* search, as in most of

their salvage operations, all radio messages had been dispatched in code.

For half a day the Dutch skipper weighed the possibilities, then he too concluded that *Leicester* had probably gone down.

Zwarte Zee held to her course for Hamilton.

Josephine and *Lillian* continued to course the wilderness of ocean like two black hounds. The gale began to slacken during the late afternoon of the 18th and both tugs returned to maximum speed. All day the searchers scanned the empty sea until even the tug crews, professional optimists as most of them were, could no longer hide their doubts.

Early in the evening, when Cowley heard that there would be no aircraft assistance in the search, he concluded that it was time to call a halt. At 2000 hours he radioed Halifax:

> WIND N BY E FORCE 6 STILL ROUGH SEA AND SWELL VESSEL ROLLING AND PITCHING HEAVILY JOSEPHINE AND LILLIAN HAVE NOW SEARCHED 9000 SQUARE MILES WITHOUT AVAIL STOP WILL MAKE ANOTHER RADAR SWEEP TONIGHT TO SOUTHWARD BUT FEAR CASUALTY HAS FOUNDERED IN HEAVY SEAS STOP ASKED ALL SHIPPING KEEP LOOKOUT AND REPORT BUT NOTHING DOING STOP CONSIDER WASTE OF FUEL CONTINUE SEARCH AFTER TOMORROW DO YOU CONCUR

Cowley got no answer that night. In Halifax, Featherstone's position was becoming increasingly untenable—but still he refused to make the decision to call off the search.

Darkness swept the heaving seas. *Josephine*'s First Mate, Wally Myalls, relieved Third Mate Freddie Squires at the radar scope. Far off to the starboard, Wally could see the little blip which was the *Lillian*. For the rest, the screen was empty of everything except the clutter of shifting lights reflected back from the crests of breaking seas.

Time passed, and Myalls' eyes began to feel the strain. He turned away from the scope to rest them and to chat for a minute with Cowley who had come up on the bridge. Then he returned to his sepulchral watch in the hood of the machine.

Suddenly he tensed. Far to the south there was a blip that did not fade as the wave echoes faded. He stared at it for several minutes.

"Captain!" he called. "I've got something."

Instantly Cowley was at his side. Myalls stepped clear and Cowley's hands rested lightly on the control dials as he peered into the hood. Without raising his head he gave an order to the helmsman.

"Starboard twenty degrees!"

Josephine began to swing on to the new course, and everywhere aboard her men became alert. The big tug had only just turned on one of the legs of her search pattern; if she was now altering so soon it could only mean that the bridge had spotted something.

The little green blip on the face of the scope grew steadier, renewed by each sweep of the search beam. Cowley watched it with unwavering intensity. Five minutes—ten—fifteen—and then his shoulders sagged.

"It's a ship all right, Wally. But she's under way. It's not the *Leicester*."

Josephine returned to her course. The night drew on.

At 0720 hours the next morning *Lillian* came on the air by radio-telephone. For what Crowe had to say, there was no need to use the Company code.

"We've just passed through a thin oil slick," he told Cowley, "and some floating wreckage—planks, some barrels and a ripped life preserver. I think she's gone."

At 0900 September 19th, this information lay in front of Featherstone. The big man's jaw set firmer and he worked his cigar brutally between his teeth. Then, with a reluctance which amounted to physical distaste, he picked up his pencil. When he began writing, he pressed down so hard that the lead snapped with a tiny sharp report.

> FOUNDATION HALIFAX TO FOUNDATION
> JOSEPHINE IF CASUALTY NOT LOCATED
> BY NOON JOSEPHINE PROCEED NORTH
> SYDNEY LILLIAN PROCEED HALIFAX—
> FETER

Three hours later *Josephine* began to swing. When her head had steadied on her new course, Cowley wearily stretched out his hand and shut off the radar set. The search was over.

CHAPTER 2

While *Lillian* was streaking for Halifax—every man aboard her with his fingers crossed, and an eye cocked apprehensively on the door of Sparkie's shack—and while *Josephine* headed for North Sydney, another vessel was about to claim the attention of Foundation Maritime.

She was the 5000-ton Greek collier *Orion,* en route from Sydney to Botwood on the northeast coast of Newfoundland with a cargo of soft coal.

Orion was typical of a class—or family perhaps—of vessels notorious the world over. With their predilection for antiquities the Greeks had, over the years, collected under their flag some of the most ancient, worn-out, and misbegotten vessels of all time. When a ship flying some other flag finally grew so old and rickety that she was only fit for the shipbreaker's yard, chances were always good that some Greek skipper would come along and buy her for a song. Sometimes he would have financial help from his officers who were often his sons or sons-in-law. The old ship would then become very much a family affair. Her cabins would be filled to overflowing with buxom wives and numerous children. Any available clear space on her deck would sprout pens for sheep, goats, chickens, and even a cow or two. She would become, in the best usage of the word, a true ocean-going tramp beating her way around the world; going wherever she could get a cargo, and taking that cargo wherever its owner wanted it delivered.

Orion had not been home to Greece for two full years. To trace her course over those years would be to imitate the Odyssey; but on the next-to-final lap of her wanderings she had come to Sydney looking for a cargo, and she had found one there.

She was so old that no one admitted to a knowledge of her birth date. Rust had eaten her plates paper-thin, and her ancient Scotch boiler and triple-expansion engine really deserved a place in some museum on the Clyde. Still, the engine worked, and *Orion* plodded about the oceans at a laborious eight knots.

She was working up through the Straits of Belle Isle on the night of September 19th when the gale which had plagued the two salvage tugs overtook her. The waters she was sailing were narrow, and renowned for their inhospitality to vessels during heavy weather. *Orion* had no radar, of course, and her ancient radio transmitter was hardly of much more use than a crystal set. Her people presumably possessed a chart of Belle Isle Straits but, if they did, it did not prove of much service to them.

Wallowing and snorting through the storm like a water buffalo, the aged vessel was almost up to Flower Island in the Straits when she found herself attempting to take a short-cut through the land behind that island. She was not up to it. There was an ugly sound of crumpling iron plates, followed by an outraged uproar from the chickens, the sheep, and the vessel's cow.

But *Orion* was so low-powered, and had so little way on her, that even running into a cliff could not do her any mortal damage; and at dawn on the 20th she was able to back off the shore under her own steam.

She was afloat again, but her people were in something of a quandary: her forward hold was taking water and the soft coal was turning to slush in the bilges and clogging the bilge pumps. Worse still, the coal was heating up by spontaneous combustion—and had probably been doing so ever since she sailed from Sydney. The influx of salt water after the collision with the shore simply hastened the process, and wisps of smoke together with a strong smell of coal gas were soon seeping out from under her forward hatches.

Some of the crew now began looking back wistfully at the land from which they had so recently parted company. When, shortly after 0900 hours, the forehatch blew off with a resounding WHUMPH and smoke began to pour from the opening, her Captain promptly headed *Orion* back for the familiar rocks.

That Captain was an unfortunate man. When he wanted to stay in deep water he ran into the land. Now that he wished to run his ship ashore and beach her, he ran her hard on an off-lying reef nearly a mile from shore.

Shortly after she hit the reef, *Orion*'s radio officer managed to transmit an s o s. At 1030 hours Foundation Maritime in Halifax received the following cable from their agents in St John's, Newfoundland:

GREEK STEAMER ORION 5000 GROSS TONS CARGO COAL SYDNEY BOTWOOD REPORTED AGROUND FLOWER ISLAND SHIP ON FIRE CREW ABANDONING

Featherstone immediately checked *Orion*'s antecedents in the biblical-looking *Lloyd's Register of Shipping*. He was not impressed. Still, a ship in trouble is a ship in trouble, and Foundation boasted that it had never failed to do its best for any ship that needed help. A message went out to *Josephine*—then some hundred and fifty miles away from Sydney—telling Cowley to divert at once and proceed to *Orion*'s rescue. By noon *Josephine* had altered course to pass through the Cabot Straits, bound for Belle Isle.

The distance was about thirty-five hours' steaming at full speed for *Josephine*. By late evening of the 21st she raised Flower Island Light and her people could dimly see the unprepossessing hulk of the *Orion* sitting forlornly on the offshore reefs.

There was no time to be lost. Exposed from every side to wind and sea, *Orion* could not hope to survive even a moderate blow. Although it was now almost pitch dark, Cowley brought *Josephine* in as close as he dared, feeling his way with the echo sounder through the "sunkers" —the appropriate name which Newfoundlanders give to underwater reefs and rocks. A quick inspection showed that *Orion* was aground for half her length and that she was open to the sea in at least two of her holds.

Cowley and his salvage foreman, diver Ray Squires, were doubtful that the vessel would have sufficient value left in her, even if she were freed, to meet the salvage costs—but they prepared to do their best. A Lloyd's Open Form agreement was signed by the two captains.

At dawn *Josephine* was eased through the reefs and made fast alongside *Orion*. The salvors, fighting their way through a mob of sheep which had broken out of their pen during the general excitement, and brushing aside an angry flutter of cockerels, began swinging their gear aboard.

Three big gasoline pumps came first, and these were soon discharging streams of black and stinking water over the side. At the same time, two clam buckets were swung out of *Josephine*'s hold and deposited on *Orion*'s deck. Using the casualty's own derricks and winches—she still had steam—these clams were then put to work jettisoning coal out of Numbers 3 and 4 holds in order to lighten the ship.

Simultaneously, fire hoses were run from *Josephine*'s bulk CO_2 tanks to *Orion*'s Number 1 hold, and the fire was soon smothered.

The old vessel's decks had become a scene of thundering, clanging, rattling, baa-a-a-a-ing and mooing activity.

Jettisoning of coal continued but there was a heavy swell running and *Orion*'s old plates were being steadily crumpled against the reefs. Not even the big eight-inch salvage pumps could lower the water in her holds significantly, and by early afternoon it began to look like a losing battle—so much that the Captain of the *Orion* eventually shrugged his shoulders, made a sweeping gesture which seemed to convey that he was washing his hands of the whole affair, then went ashore—for good.

By 1500 hours the wind had begun to rise out of the west and shortly thereafter *Josephine* had to cast off and feel her way back out to deeper water, where she anchored. Cowley had left his Third Mate, Freddie Squires (Ray Squires' brother), and five salvage men aboard the *Orion,* with twenty or thirty Newfoundland fishermen who had been hired to assist. A dozen of *Orion's* crew and all the livestock also remained aboard.

Within an hour it was evident that the westerly was going to blow up into a full gale. At this juncture the fishermen politely announced they were going home to Flower Cove while they were able. They climbed into their one-lung motor skiffs and putted away through the surf which was already beginning to break on the nearby reefs. With their departure, as Squires said afterwards, he began to feel a little lonely.

"The gale got up remarkably fast. By seven o'clock it was blowing Force 8 or 9 and the sea was breaking white all around us. We could see *Josephine* was dragging her anchors and was in trouble herself. She got one hook up but the other jammed in the rocks and she finally had to cut the cable and abandon it. Then she steamed out to sea. There was nothing else for her to do. She couldn't have come anywhere near us, drawing the water she did, and to have stayed close to the coast in a howling westerly would have been plain foolishness.

"After she pulled out we felt twice as lonely. We had no boats and anyway ordinary ships' boats couldn't have lived in the sea that was breaking right across the *Orion.*

"The Greeks began to get awfully nervous. They kept asking me to use the radio to call *Josie* back. When I wouldn't, they began to jump up and down and shout. I didn't want to drown any more than they did—but *Josie* couldn't have helped us anyway.

"Buck Dassylva, he was our pumpman aboard, came on deck to tell me the whole bottom was going out of the ship and the engine room was flooding. We hustled down there right quick and put out the fires. All we needed to make things really interesting just about then was a good boiler explosion.

"When we put out the fires, the Greeks seemed to think that was the end, and they started chasing me round and round the ship trying to get me to perform a miracle on the radio.

"I couldn't understand the Greeks very well, but I tell you, I *could* outrun them. Of course there were a lot of obstacles. Every now and again I'd fall over a sheep or goat, and Buck would laugh like hell. I think he was making book on me.

"Meantime Cowley had sent out a general s o s for help, and he got an answer from a Newfoundland revenue cutter, the *Marvita*, which was lying in Flower Cove to shelter from the gale. She was a shallow-draught boat and her skipper, Captain Houndsel, was a real old-time New-foundlander, the kind that is supposed to be half seal. It was a good thing for us he was around, because he was probably the only man on that whole coast who would have dared to try and get us off the *Orion*.

"About ten o'clock even the Greeks had given up, and none of us thought the future looked very bright. *Orion* was breaking up under us and we figured she couldn't last much longer. Then, all of a sudden, a searchlight cut through the storm, and a blinker light started up.

"I got hold of a flashlight and answered back. It was Houndsel in the *Marvita*, and he signalled that he was going to try and pick his way right through those shoals—they were breaking white as milk—and pick us up.

"He warned us to be ready. 'Will lie alongside for sixty seconds,' he signalled. He wouldn't have dared stay longer, and I don't know yet how he risked putting her alongside *Orion* at all.

"I had everybody lined up at the rail waiting for him when he flashed another signal: 'Don't come empty handed.'

"I knew what he meant. *Orion* had more booze aboard her than Halifax could have drunk in a week. I hustled around and got every man to tuck a couple of bottles into his jacket or his shirt. Sort of passage money you might say. Remembering that *Marvita* was a revenue boat, I only hoped Houndsel had left the revenue officers behind in Flower Cove.

"Houndsel brought the *Marvita* in like a bird. She just touched alongside, and everyone was aboard of her in one jump, and then Houndsel was backing her out to sea. About then some of the bottles just seemed to pop open by themselves.

"When we got clear we made a rough passage around to Flower Cove. As we were going into the harbour, I could hear what sounded like a hundred motor boats staring up. Houndsel switched on the searchlight, and there was every boat in Flower Cove that had a motor and would float at all, heading out to sea.

"Can you imagine it! A Force 9 gale on a lee shore, and those little skiffs were heading right out into it. I couldn't figure what was going on so I asked Houndsel. He just grinned and said, 'Well, Bye, y'know the *Orion's* abandoned now.' He didn't need to say another word.

"Next morning the gale had pretty well blown itself out and I went back to the wreck to see about the gear we had left on board. She really *was* a wreck by then. Completely broken, and a total loss—and stripped as clean as a whistle! Those fishermen hadn't left a thing to go to waste—not even the cow.

"I couldn't for the life of me figure how they got the cow off of her. So I asked one of the local boys, as a special favour, to tell me how they managed to get a cow into a skiff in that kind of a storm.

"He said, 'We never put her in no skiff. She'd have sunk it, and us too. We just ties a rope around her horns and kicks her overboard, and when she gets clear of the reefs we picks up the free end of the line and swims her home!' "

When Squires and his salvage men got back to *Josephine,* they found a wildly impatient Cowley waiting for them. Almost before they could step aboard their ship from the *Marvita,* the tug was under way.

While Squires had been involved aboard the *Orion,* a startling encounter had been taking place a thousand miles away to the southeast.

PART SIX

CHAPTER 1

THE low-power steamer track between North America and the mouth of the Mediterranean is one of the busiest of the North Atlantic routes. Scores of ships may be found along its length on any given day. Because of the heavy traffic, ships following the track do not necessarily adhere exactly to this invisible ocean highway along the 36th parallel of lattitude.

The French steamer *Gien*, westbound from Marseilles for Baltimore, was one of those which chose to parallel the track, but farther north. She was in fact running close to the 37th parallel when her Master shot the sun at noon on the 21st and found he was still 1400 miles away from making his American landfall.

It was a warm and sunny day, and the slow pounding of *Gien*'s engines had a soporific effect upon the crew. Perhaps the lookout was dozing just a little. At any rate, when he finally did see the object looming hard on the starboard bow it was already close at hand. His astonished shout brought the watch officer to the wing of the bridge with his binoculars. For a long minute he stared, then he called his Captain.

Gien woke up in a hurry. Men came scrambling out of the cabins and the forecastle and climbed to points of vantage all over the ship, staring with rank incredulity at the apparition which had appeared ahead of them. *Gien*'s course was quickly altered and she drew slowly up to the monstrosity which rode the sunlit seas.

It was a ship—a big ship—lying so far over that she appeared to be floating on her side. Her whole bottom, to below the starboard bilge keel, lay exposed to the gaze of *Gien*'s people.

Gien circled the silent apparition somewhat warily. It

was apparent that she was totally abandoned and derelict. Someone read the name on her stern. LEICESTER—LONDON.

Gien's people were filled with a mixture of awe and downright cupidity. Her Master would have liked nothing better than to put a line on the derelict and tow her into Baltimore so that he could claim salvage on her. But . . . he had his own ship to think about. Baltimore was 1400 miles away, and the morning weather had included the report of a new hurricane—Hurricane VIII—which was even then nearing Key West in Florida, and which could be expected to roar northward across the western approaches during the next few days. There were other things to consider too. One of these was the extreme hazard, if not impossibility, of putting a boarding crew aboard the wreck. A second was the conviction among the men looking at her that no ship with a list as bad as *Leicester's* could possibly stay afloat for very long, even in relatively gentle weather.

With a sigh, *Gien's* thrifty Breton Master reluctantly gave the order to put his ship back on course; and as *Leicester* grew smaller on the eastern horizon he dispatched a message to the New York Coast Guard:

> PASSED SHIPWRECKED STEAMER LEICESTER LIBERTY SHIP FROM LONDON 3707 NORTH 5214 WEST SHIP ABANDONED 60 DEGREE LISTED DRIFT NORTHEAST VERY DANGEROUS FOR NAVIGATION

When a copy of *Gien's* message reached Featherstone through the agency of Air/Sea Rescue, at 1300 hours on the 21st, there was hell to pay.

The Salvage Master did not demean himself by saying "I told you so," but his pale blue eyes were as hard as rocks as he strode through Foundation's offices issuing his orders. They were *his* orders too. He had assumed command, and not a voice was raised to question him.

Featherstone was in an awkward position. His biggest and best tug, the *Josephine*, was committed to the *Orion*

—a job which, even if successful, would not do much more than return the costs of the operation. *Lillian* was still six hours out of Halifax and could not be turned about at sea since her stores and her supplies of fuel were all but exhausted. She would have to come on to port, refuel, and then go out again—if she was able. Her overworked engines were causing trouble and she was badly in need of a refit.

The lack of tug equipment was not the only problem. There was Hurricane VIII as well.

Born in the Caribbean a hundred miles south of Jamaica on the 18th of September, at first a rather puny cyclone, it had rapidly taken on strength and stature as it curved northward. During the night of the 20th-21st it had struck Cuba, doing extensive shore damage, killing several people and driving three big ships ashore. By noon on the 21st, it had reached Key West. There it had blown away the U.S. Weather Bureau's anemometers after registering a velocity of 120 miles per hour and driving the steamship *Ocean Wave* ashore.

The pressure of a massive Continental High lying over the Atlantic seaboard made it logical to anticipate that the new cyclone would curve northeastward after leaving Florida. If it should pass anywhere in the vicinity of the *Leicester*, it could be assumed that it would finish her. Even if it did not go her way, it would certainly pose a substantial hazard to any tugs that might be running east in search of her.

Meanwhile there was little that Featherstone could actually do save pace his office and think about *Leicester* herself. A score of times he checked her position on the chart. Each time he did so he was confronted by a conundrum. *Gien's* Master had said the derelict was drifting to the northeast. But Featherstone had a long and intimate knowledge of those waters and he knew that the prevailing winds and currents in *Leicester's* vicinity almost invariably set to the southeast. Since it would take nearly three days before one of his tugs could reach the search area, there would be ample time for *Leicester* to drift an additional 100 to 200 miles—depending on the strength of wind and current. This being the case, it was imperative to direct the tugs along the correct line of drift.

Reason dictated that Featherstone should accept *Gien*'s statement and plan the tugs' courses accordingly. But experience and intuition told him differently. . . .

Gien's message was received in New York at 1240 hours Atlantic Standard Time. Half an hour later it was rebroadcast to all ships in the western approaches as a special warning of navigation hazards. By early afternoon hardly a vessel in the western section of the North Atlantic had not heard the news.

One of the vessels which heard it—and with particular interest—was the Dutch tug *Zwarte Zee*. She was then entering New York Harbour with the dead tow she had brought in from Bermuda. Despite the almost superhuman efforts of her crew, it was not until 1600 hours that the *Zwarte Zee* could get rid of her tow, refill her tanks with diesel oil, and put back to sea.

Her Master had reconsidered his earlier belief that *Leicester* could not remain afloat. That she *had* remained afloat since her abandonment five days earlier meant there was a reasonable chance she would stay afloat until she was found. And, with immense good luck, she might be eased into the nearest port. Allowing for the interval between *Gien*'s sighting of the derelict and the time *Zwarte Zee* could expect to reach the scene, the Dutch skipper laid off *Leicester*'s probable drift—in a northeasterly direction. Then he laid out his own course toward *Leicester*'s estimated position in sixty hours' time.

Zwarte Zee cleared Ambrose Light at 1800 hours September 21st. She had a thousand miles to go.

She did not sail unnoticed. In the salvage business an efficient intelligence service is vital—and Foundation's cloak-and-dagger work was excellent. Before *Zwarte Zee* was out of sight of land, Featherstone received a telephone call from New York and knew that he had a formidable rival in the race to reach the *Leicester*.

At 1732 hours on the 21st, *Foundation Lillian* had Halifax Harbour approach buoy abeam, and her people were beginning to relax. They could already look through the entrance to the harbour, and beyond to the wooded ridges with their aura of sunny contentment. Most of the off-duty men had packed their seabags and were discussing how and where they would spend their leave ashore.

At 1900 hours *Lillian*'s lines were secured to Foundation's dock and Crowe rang down to tell Chief Engineer Higgins that he was finished with the engines. Then he picked up his suitcase, walked off the bridge and came down to the main deck where the gangplank was being run ashore.

The plank had barely touched the dock before Featherstone started up it. He met Crowe at the rail.

"*Leicester*'s been sighted," he said abruptly. "You'll refuel at once at Imperoyal. Your stores are waiting here in the salvage shed. *Zwarte Zee* sailed from New York three hours ago. She's got four or five knots' speed on you—but she's got farther to go. I want you cleared and on your way by ten P.M."

There is no printable record of the reaction of *Lillian*'s crew. But they were salvage men.

At 2207 hours September 21st, *Foundation Lillian* let slip her lines, backed into the stream, and headed out to sea. She had been just three hours in home port.

The morning of the 22nd broke cloudy with light southwest winds as *Lillian* drove southeast at her best speed of fourteen knots. Down below, her Chief Engineer watched the diesels apprehensively. Higgins had much to worry about. *Lillian*'s engines had been giving trouble almost since the day she joined Foundation's fleet They were good enough engines but too delicate for the hard, sustained labour which was a deep-sea salvage vessel's lot; and they had become increasingly temperamental during the past few months. Higgins kept his fingers crossed and listened intently for the first indication of trouble in the ear-splitting hubbub of thirty-two thundering cylinders.

Lillian was observing radio silence, and apart from

reporting her noon position to Halifax in code she transmitted no messages that day. This was a routine precaution. It was always possible for a rival tug, using directional antennae, to take a bearing on *Lillian's* transmissions and, from a series of such "DF" bearings, deduce the course and possibly the plans of the Foundation tug.

Zwarte Zee also maintained absolute silence and *Lillian's* Sparkie did not hear the Dutch tug's call sign once, although he was now on permanent listening watch.

Far to the north, out of direct contact with Halifax Radio, *Josephine's* people were labouring to save the ancient *Orion*. As yet they did not know of *Leicester's* apparent resurrection from the ocean grave.

Far to the south, Hurricane VIII was behaving in a most unusual manner. For nearly forty hours it had remained almost motionless over the Florida peninsula: "motionless" in terms of forward movement. There was nothing motionless about its circling winds which did $12,000,-000 worth of damage to the Tourist State.

Of *Leicester* herself there was no further word. Merchant ships following the central track had no desire to encounter the derelict, particularly at night, and many of them had drastically altered course to let her have this section of the ocean to herself.

That she was still a serious menace to navigation was recognized that afternoon by the United States Coast Guard, which determined to send a long-range aircraft to locate her and keep her under surveillance until she either sank, was taken in tow, or drifted well clear of the track. But the distances from suitable airfields proved too great, and the consequent risks to the aircraft too heavy, and so the plan was dropped.

In Foundation's offices at Halifax, every member of the staff held a watching brief. Lights burned until after midnight. Those of the operations people who went to their own homes slept lightly, half-listening for the ring of the telephone.

At 2300 hours a message from *Josephine* was delivered to Featherstone:

ORION POUNDING HEAVILY IN FULL NORTHEAST GALE HOLDS STOKEHOLD ENGINE ROOM FLOODED HAD TO LET GO AND CLEAR AWAY FROM REEFS STOP CREW AND SIX MY MEN ABANDONED CASUALTY IN REVENUE BOAT WILL TRY RECOVER OUR GEAR IN MORNING STOP CONSIDER NO VALUE LEFT IN ORION

Half an hour later a coded reply was crackling through the night air from Halifax Radio to St. John's Radio, which relayed it on.

ABANDON GEAR PROCEED EARLIEST LEICESTER STILL AFLOAT ASSIST LILLIAN SEARCHING AREA SOUTHEAST 3707 N 5214 W ALL REPEAT ALL COMMUNICATIONS CODE—FETER

"Searching area *southeast* . . ." Featherstone had made his decision. He was ignoring the information which *Gien*'s Master had reported concerning *Leicester*'s drift.

CHAPTER 2

By noon on September 23rd three salvage tugs were racing toward the last known position of the derelict. *Lillian* was about 250 miles northwest of *Leicester*'s position as reported by *Gien*. *Josephine*, foaming along at her best of almost seventeen knots down the west coast of Newfoundland, still had more than 900 miles to go. As for *Zwarte Zee*—she had remained as silent as the grave. The Foundation tugboat masters, as well as the anxious men in Halifax, could only guess at her location.

No one needed to guess at the location of Hurricane VIII. Late on the 22nd, the centre had begun to move very rapidly toward the east-northeast. By noon on the 23rd, it was 300 miles off the Florida coast, heading directly for Bermuda—after having pummelled the British M/V *Stanhall* to the point where she had been forced to head for port in a near-sinking condition.

A projection of the hurricane's track now pointed straight to the area where *Leicester* was believed to be. It seemed that a fourth participant had joined the race.

The 24th broke grey and stormy over the western approaches. Bucking heavy seas and a Force 5 wind from southerly, *Lillian* was a tense ship as the morning lengthened. Before noon she was passing *Leicester's* position as reported by *Gien* on the 21st. But more than seventy hours had elapsed since then, and *Leicester* might have gone down or she might have drifted anywhere within an easterly arc of 90 degrees, for a distance of up to 200 miles. The fact that no other vessel had reported her during this long interval made the prospects of her still being afloat seem dim. Even if she *was* afloat, *Lillian's* people knew that *Zwarte Zee*, a ship of nearly twice *Lillian's* displacement and with a turn of speed four or five knots greater, must also have arrived in the search area. And *Zwarte Zee* had radar: *Lillian* did not. The odds heavily favoured the big Dutch tug.

The suspense was not eased by Higgins' report to the bridge that he was having trouble with the starboard engine. *Lillian's* speed had fallen off to thirteen knots, and Crowe now had the choice of accepting what might be an even greater reduction in speed or of allowing the engines to be stopped entirely while repairs were made. He chose to keep *Lillian* going and, obeying Featherstone's instructions, he began searching a fifty-mile-wide swath of ocean to the southeast.

There was only one bright spot during that morning: the weather report. Hurricane VIII had inexplicably changed course again and was now heading northeastward, well away from the search area. The news cheered *Lillian's* people—but it did not cheer Captain Cowley on the *Josephine*.

At 1720 hours Cowley, then nearly abeam of Sydney once again, received the following from Halifax Radio:

> AT 1530 CENTRE ATLANTIC HURRICANE 400 MILES NORTH OF BERMUDA MOVING NORTHEAST AT 32 KNOTS HURRICANE WINDS COVER AREA 50 MILES IN CENTRE AND GALES AS FAR AS 300 MILES FROM CENTRE STOP CONTINUED NORTHEAST MOVEMENT WITH SOME ACCELERATION IN FORWARD MOTION IS EXPECTED THROUGH NEXT 24 HOURS

Having made up its mind to go northeast, Hurricane VIII was wasting no time about it. At 32 knots its predicted path put it on a collision course with *Josephine*, with the collision due to occur about dawn of the 25th.

Cowley's dilemma was not eased by a subsequent message from Featherstone:

> HURRICANE MOVING NE LIKELY PASS SOUTH SABLE ISLAND TAKE ACTION AVOID CENTRE BUT CONSIDER COMPETING SALVAGE VESSEL NOW BELIEVED SEARCH AREA

That settled it. A trifle grimly Cowley gave the order to batten down ship for heavy weather; and he held his course.

Aboard the *Lillian*, as storm murk shrank the visible world, there was hardly a man of the deck crew whose eyes were not sore and aching from straining to the far horizons for sight of the abandoned ship; but the watchers had seen nothing save the unending seas. They had not glimpsed what they dreaded most—the squat superstructure of *Zwarte Zee;* nor had they seen so much as a curl of smoke from any merchant ship which might conceivably have had a clue to give.

Sparkie clung to his radio like a man in love, listening

to the ship-to-ship chatter of vessels scattered over half of the Atlantic, and waiting for some word. At 1800 hours, international code started to clatter out of the speaker over his head. His hand jumped to the message pad.

I BBB SS ALBISOLA TO ALL SHIPS AND USCG 1740 AST SIGHTED ABANDONED FLOATING LIBERTY SHIP 3600 NORTH 4930 WEST—SIGNED MASTER

Within minutes Crowe had plotted the position on his chart. It was 155 miles *southeast* of the position given by the *Gien. Lillian,* which had been following a complicated rectilinear search pattern, was still a little more than 90 miles from the point of the new sighting. Now she turned abruptly on the direct course, like a hound with a hot scent blowing in her nostrils.

In the engine room Higgins had worked a small miracle by managing to effect partial repairs with the engines still running. In response to the news from the bridge, he ran both engines up to maximum revolutions, and held his breath. . . .

Zwarte Zee may perhaps not have heard the original call from the *Albisola,* but she must certainly have heard a notice to Mariners broadcast from New York three hours later, containing the gist of *Albisola*'s message. And by 2300 hours she too must have been racing toward that intangible point on the ocean's surface, with all the speed her 3000-horsepower engines could provide.

The night drew down, overcast and threatening. *Lillian,* rolling heavily in the chop which was building with a rising southerly wind, was taking water over her bows and drenching wheelhouse and bridge. No one seemed to notice. On both bridge wings oilskin-clad figures stared into the murk ahead.

Lillian drove hard all night against a gathering sea and rising wind, and by dawn she was in such heavy weather that she was forced to reduce speed. Nevertheless by

1100 hours on the morning of the 25th she had reached
the position given by the *Albisola*. There was nothing
to mark the spot, and no indication of where *Leicester*
might have gone, except for the wind, which had now
shifted a little more westerly. Judging solely by the wind,
Leicester should have drifted in a generally easterly or
northeasterly direction during the night But it was not
the wind which was determining her drift—it was the
ocean current; and the current in this vicinity was running
almost due south. Crowe set up a new search pattern—
again directed into the southeast.

It is difficult to know what happened to *Zwarte Zee*
that day; but since it was her Master's known intention
to search northeast of the *Gien*'s sighting, it is possible
to reconstruct what probably occurred.

Since she had radar, she would have been able to steam
straight into the northeast from the *Gien* position instead
of having to follow a zigzagging visual-search pattern.
By the time her Master heard the notice to Mariners
retailing the *Albisola* sighting, *Zwarte Zee* was probably
about 200 miles north of the newly reported position of
the *Leicester*, in a portion of the Western Ocean where
the current normally sets almost due east. This set, combined with a strong southwesterly wind, would almost
certainly have influenced the Dutch Captain to lay out
an interception course designed to close with *Leicester*,
in about twelve hours, at a point sixty or seventy miles
northeast of the position reported by the *Albisola*.

In any event *Lillian*'s crew, who were momentarily expecting to raise *Zwarte Zee*, saw nothing of the Dutch
tug during the intense hours of the 25th. But then, they
saw nothing of the *Leicester* either. As one of the salvage
gang remarked:

"Talk about looking for a needle in a haystack—that's
nothing to trying to find a ship that may be anywhere on
about ten thousand square miles of the Atlantic. Some
of the lads even took to climbing the foremast to try
and see a little farther. With the visibility we had that
day we couldn't see much more than five or six miles

from the bridge. And one of the men damn near got hove
clean into the ocean when we took a roll that laid the old
girl right over on her side.

"The crew had begun to figure either we were jinxed
or the *Leicester* was another Flying Dutchman. For about
the tenth time since the first search started on the 17th,
we began to think she'd gone down. But every time we'd
figured that before, damned if she hadn't shown up again.
Rose claimed she didn't *want* anyone to find her—that
she liked being on her own and planned to stay that way.
I tell you, there were some hard thoughts about her on
our boat that day . . ."

At 1400 hours, one of the lookouts suddenly spotted
something off to port. *Lillian* swung hungrily over to have
a look, but it was only a mess of flotsam consisting of some
shattered boards and a rusty iron barrel.

As dusk came down again, effectively blinding *Lillian*
through the long night watches, there was a growing
conviction that *Leicester* must have sunk or that *Zwarte
Zee* must have found her and taken her in tow for land.
It seemed incredible that the big Dutchman, with his
radar eyes, could have failed to find the ship if she was
still afloat. But on the other hand, there had still been
not a single call from *Zwarte Zee*'s radio, and if she *had*
found the prize and laid a claim to it, she might have
been expected to tell the world about it.

The 25th was an uneventful day for *Lillian*'s people, but
not so for *Josephine*. During the night of the 24th-25th,
Josephine held to her chosen course, driving at full speed
and refusing to be bluffed into slowing down or altering
course by a mere hurricane.

Cowley was banking on the probability that the hurricane would cross his bows far enough in advance so that
his tug would miss the centre of the Serpent's Coil. But
as the night drew on, grew dark as death, and began to
thunder to the voice of the rising winds, he was not so
sure. By 2200 hours *Josie* was taking solid water over
her high bows, and the state of the yeasty sea was mak-

ing it quite clear that, if it was a fight she wanted, she would get all that she could stomach.

Yielding a little valour to discretion, Cowley slowed her down to three-quarters speed—but kept her on her course.

Salvage men seldom use superlatives when they discuss a storm at sea—if indeed they can be persuaded to discuss it at all—but many of those aboard the *Josephine* have lasting memories of this night. One crewman came close to waxing lyrical about it—in a grim sort of way.

"She wasn't no boat at all by then—she was a bloody airplane what couldn't quite take off. I never see nothing like it in twenty-seven years at sea. I got into Sparkie's cabin and he was going crazy chasing his trunk around the room. Every now and then they'd change sides and the trunk would chase him for a bit. I got up on his bunk, jammed my feet against the deck, and braced my elbows between the bunkboard and the bulkhead. In between laughing my fool head off at Sparkie, I began to feel a wee bit peaked-like. Not scared so much as just plain cowardly. My God, she rolled! And pitched! When she come down off a crest she must have been putting her bows right under. I didn't go on deck to see. I didn't like it where I was, but I knew I wouldn't like it any better up on top."

This was a rare outburst from a seaman of the salvage tugs. It stands in revealing contrast to the brief entries in the ship's log for that night:

> 2345 *Reduced to three quarter speed. Wind and sea rising. Glass falling steadily.*
> 2400 *Reduced speed to half. Vessel rolling and pitching heavily. Wind veered east-south-east Force 10. Heavy seas and swell.*

"Vessel rolling and pitching heavily": it rings like a litany through the logs of the salvage vessels.

By noon of the 25th, *Josephine* was clear of the worst of it. Salt-stained to the trucks of her masts, she was ploughing through the after-swells at a full sixteen knots, but she was still 400 miles short of the *Albisola*'s position for *Leicester*.

On the morning of the 26th, the general atmospheric disturbance kicked up by the passage of the hurricane brought heavy weather and high seas to the whole search area. It brought no pleasure to the gloomy crew of the *Lillian*, and could hardly have eased the mood of *Zwarte Zee*'s people either.

In Halifax, even Featherstone was beginning to get edgy. The strain had communicated itself to the head office of the parent company in Montreal, where vice-presidents were nervously accosting one another to ask if there was any news. It was no longer simply a matter of a million-dollar salvage operation—the whole *Leicester* affair had now assumed the stature of a major maritime mystery. But no one in Foundation Maritime had any thought of calling off the search—least of all Featherstone, whose pugnacious lower jaw kept thrusting out farther and farther as the hours passed.

"He'd got to the point," said one of his associates, "that if *Leicester* had gone down, he would have wanted to try to raise her from the ocean floor. Getting that boat had become the only thing he thought about. Each time there was a call from Halifax Radio we dreaded to hear the news, for fear *Zwarte Zee* had made the find. If that had happened, I really believe Feathers would have stolen a destroyer from the Navy and gone out and taken *Leicester* away from the Dutchman by brute force."

At 1000 hours on the 26th there was a flurry aboard *Lillian* when the lookout reported a ship on the horizon to the south. It was soon obvious that it could not be the derelict, for this ship was under way. Crowe veered toward her at full speed anyway. There was always a chance the stranger might have something to report. *Lillian* bore down upon her—unwilling to use her radio because of the *Zwarte Zee*—and shortly before noon came within hailing distance of the Norwegian Steamship *Elg*. The *Elg*'s people were amazed by the mid-ocean encounter. Such a little boat, so far at sea. What could she be doing? Crowe soon told them but they, alas, could tell him nothing in return. They had seen no sign of an abandoned ship.

Reluctantly *Lillian* turned back to resume her search pattern. She had a beaten look about her that was reflected in the faces of her people. They had almost given up hope of ever putting their ship on dock in Halifax.

"We figured," said one of the engineers, "to be out there for twenty-five days, that was our fuel endurance. And then we figured to go on drifting for the rest of time, just like the *Leicester*. We knew damn well Feathers would never let us come ashore without her!"

As the southing increased, it grew hotter aboard the tug. Men were stripping off the heavy jackets they had worn in northern waters, and sweat was flowing freely from the helmsman's face.

It was nearly 1300 on the 26th and Crowe was considering whether to go below for a bite to eat when Sparkie burst out of his shack. He took the steps to the chart house almost at a leap and thrust a scribbled message into the Captain's hand. The message had been transmitted in clear and every other vessel within hundreds of miles must have received it at the same instant *Lillian* had.

SS JAMES MCHENRY AT 1235 SIGHTED DERELICT VESSEL IN POSITION 3222 NORTH 4836 WEST VESSEL IS LEICESTER OF LONDON AND HAS A HEAVY LIST THIS VESSEL IS A MENACE TO NAVIGATION

Hastily Crowe plotted the position. It was only forty miles away—again to the southeast! Without turning from the chart he yelled the new course to the helmsman even as he was laying it out. At the same instant, Rose jumped to the voice pipe and called Higgins in the engine room.

"She's been spotted! Barely forty miles away. Oh! Chiefie! if you ever made a boat run fast, you better do it now!"

Lillian turned on her heel and they say she began to scamper through the long green swells. The drone of her diesels took on a feverish quality, and foam filled her wake even as the bone in her teeth began to swell.

It was now or never. Of a certainty *Zwarte Zee* could not be far away.

All hands lined *Lillian*'s upperworks. Monkeys' Island was so crowded it was hard to find standing room. Every eye peered forward.

The two hours which followed seemed endless. At 1510 a Newfoundlander who had climbed almost to the masthead let out a bellow that could have been heard all the way home to his native island.

"*I sees her, Byes!*"

From the bridge wing the Mate roared back:

"*Is she alone?*"

"*Lonely as an old maid in winter time!*"

The *Leicester* had been found.

PART SEVEN

"As we bore down on her nobody had a word to say. I guess most of the men never thought we'd find her, and some of us had begun to wonder if she existed at all.

"It wasn't just the end of the days and days of uncertainty that got us—it was the look of the ship herself. Nobody aboard *Lillian* had ever seen anything quite like it —and during the war most of us saw plenty of torpedoed derelicts. Torpedoed ships were always low in the water, usually half awash. But this ship stuck up until she looked damn near as big as the *Queen Mary*. She looked to me to be lying flat on her side, and right on top of the water like the great-granddaddy of the biggest whale that ever was.

"She seemed so unnatural—for a ship—that it was indecent. As we closed with her there wasn't a man who wasn't waiting for her to finish her roll and slip away down before our eyes.

"We came up from her starboard side—or maybe I should say from her bottom side, since her bilge keel was a good ten feet out of the water. As we came around her bows so we could see her decks and superstructure, I began to feel as nervous as a kid waiting for the big bang at a fireworks show. We were thinking: what in the name of God is stopping her from going over? She seemed to have about a fifty degree permanent list, but she was rolling down past seventy degrees. Each time she rolled, the seas ran in over her decks, and some broke clean above the edge of her boat deck. As we came past her port side we could almost look down her funnel.

"When I remembered that this ship had been abandoned at the tag-end of a hurricane more than ten days earlier, and had drifted derelict about six hundred miles to the southeast through three heavy storms and a lot of ordinary bad weather, I knew I was looking at some kind of sea-going miracle. Not the churchy kind, you understand, but the kind ships sometimes seem to be able to pull off on their own, without any help from men or God. This was a ship that didn't want to die."

At 1700 hours Featherstone's secretary finished decoding a message which had been received a few minutes earlier. Featherstone was not exactly hanging over her shoulder—he would not have betrayed his impatience quite so blatantly—but almost as soon as her pencil stopped moving, his big hand closed over the transcript:

> FOUNDATION HALIFAX
> LYING OFF CASUALTY HAS 50 DEGREE LIST INCREASING TO 70 DEGREES IN SWELLS STOP DOES NOT APPEAR TO BE MAKING WATER STOP WILL ATTEMPT TO BOARD TONIGHT BUT WILL NOT ATTEMPT TOW TILL EXAMINED CASUALTY STOP WILL WORK WITH JOSEPHINE CONFIRM WHO SHOULD TAKE TOW STOP NO SIGN RIVAL TUG BUT THINK NEAR AT HAND—
> CROWE

Featherstone laid the message down, dug out a cigar and carefully lit it. His only comment was: "Mmmmm. Damn near time." But the outthrust jaw no longer looked like the prow of an icebreaker and the pale blue eyes seemed almost gentle.

In his reply to Crowe, Featherstone was positively garrulous.

> GOOD WORK CONSIDER JOSEPHINE SHOULD TOW AHEAD WITH LILLIAN FREE TO GO ON LINE ASTERN TO STEER IF NEEDED COWLEY AND YOU HAVE TO DETERMINE BEST METHOD BY TRIAL STOP DETERMINE DESTINATION SIMI-

LARLY BUT CONSIDER BETTER CHANCES
FAVOURABLE WEATHER TOWARD BER-
MUDA STOP IMPERATIVE YOU GET MEN
ABOARD NOW TO AVOID CHANCES RIVAL
TUG HOOKING UP IN NIGHT—FETER

Crowe and Rose, on *Lillian*'s bridge, read the message together. A little ruefully Crowe said:

"Feathers has really let himself go, hasn't he? Actually forced himself to say 'Good work.' Well, let's get on with it."

As *Lillian* was bearing down on the derelict her crewmen had been preparing a dory and Rose had been selecting a boarding party. It was to consist of himself, Chief Engineer Higgins, and two Newfoundlanders to handle the boat. Higgins' job was to check the engine room while Rose took formal possession of the vessel.

Rose never had any trouble remembering that moment:

"We circled her twice, closing to three or four hundred yards so we could examine her and weigh the chances. She didn't look any better close up than she had at a distance. Darkness was just a couple of hours away and there was a strong wind, a very heavy sea, and an overcast sky. Not what you'd call regatta weather.

"When I'd seen all I could from *Lillian*'s bridge I told Crowe I was ready and he hove-to about a mile to wind-ward of the ship. We had the dory on our after deck and eight men picked it up bodily and heaved it over with two seamen in it. The Newfoundlanders held the dory close enough so Higgins and I could make the jump, then we pulled away for *Leicester*.

"Nobody knows how lonely the ocean can be until he takes a look at it from a sixteen-foot open boat running through seas ten to fifteen feet high. The dory may be the best sea boat ever invented, but it takes faith to believe that when you're out in one.

"The seas were heavy enough so we only got glimpses of *Leicester* and *Lillian* as we went up on the crests. They looked like toys.

"It took us about forty minutes to close with *Leicester*, and by then we'd discover we weren't alone. The sea was lousy with sharks. I suppose they'd been following *Leicester* since she was abandoned, figuring she was bound to go down, and maybe leave some tidbits floating on the surface.

"We had no time to fool around so we pulled straight in toward *Leicester*'s lee rail, just abaft her house. It didn't look good. She'd lift the lee rail fifteen feet clear of the sea, then she'd roll back and put it under. As she rolled down, the water spilled off her decks with a swoosh that would have drowned our dory.

"If we were going to get aboard at all, we had to make contact when the lee rail was coming up. There was about twenty seconds for a man to make the jump. Then the dory had to pull like blazes to get clear.

"Higgins went first. He got to the bow of the dory and balanced there while I watched our chance. As the ship began to roll up I gave a yell and the dorymen ran the boat in until her bow was about three feet from the rail. Higgins never hesitated. He caught the rail, pulled himself over it head first, and then went clawing up the deck taking advantage of the temporary reduction in the list. By the time she began to roll back he had got hold of a hatch coaming and was clear of the sea.

"I was next. I barely got wet at all. Before she could roll down I scuttled along the lee rail toward the lift of the stern. Then I hauled myself around the stern and up to the high side, going hand over hand along the rail.

"I had two flags stuffed inside my jacket—the Red Ensign and Foundation's house flag. First thing I did was haul the Red Ensign up on the after ensign mast. Then I worked forward along the high side to the bridge and hoisted the house flag. Whatever happened after that, we'd at least put our mark on *Leicester*.

"Up to then I'd been too busy to look around. After I got the house flag up I glanced down the deck toward the lee rail. She was rolling to port then and her deck was canted steeper than the average church roof. I seemed to be looking nearly fifty feet straight down into the sea. The dory was standing off about a hundred yards away, and I tell you that little boat looked good to me.

"Higgins appeared about then, and I decided we'd best get off while we could. There were some rope ends dangling down the after deck and we slid down these. Higgins was first off, and when the dory nosed in for him he made the jump without any trouble.

"The dory pulled back to wait for *Leicester* to complete her next roll, and I slid down and got up on the rail, hanging on to the stays of the after derrick mast.

"Two or three really hefty seas must have come rolling up just then, because when she went down this time she kept on going until the water was away over my head. For all I knew, she meant to go right over. I hung on tight and I remember saying to myself, 'What the hell are you doing here anyway?'

"Then she began coming up. I broke the surface, got a gulp of air, and looked around. The dory was standing off about fifty yards away, and I seemed to be looking right down the gullets of the three men aboard of her. If they'd had their mouths open any wider, a shark could have slid right down their windpipes.

"The sharks were still hanging about. I thought about them and wondered if I could make a dash for higher ground before *Leicester* put me down again. There wasn't time. Down she went, and once more she buried me right under.

"I'd had about enough of that, and the dorymen must have known it. They took an awful chance and ran right in as she came down for the third time. I jumped, and somehow landed in the boat. The four of us had to pull like hell to get clear.

"As we came around past her stern I saw that her logline was still out. We'd lost *Lillian*'s some time earlier, so I decided to salvage this one.

"We rowed aft until I could reach the line and cut it where it ran up to the ship's stern, then I began hauling in the trailing section. It was surprisingly hard work. I hauled and hauled and finally something broke water a few yards off.

"Caught on the rotator at the end of the log-line was a three-legged wooden stool. Don't ask me where it came from. But a shark had ahold of the stool, and he wasn't anxious to let go.

"We hauled him in till he was close enough to whack with an oar before he gave it up. I've still got that stool, and it still has his tooth marks on it.

"It was nearly dark by now so we headed back for *Lillian*. The shark kept us company all the way. I guess he was hoping the bottom would fall out of the dory so he'd get even. I can't figure yet what in hell he wanted with that stool."

Leicester was still derelict, but no longer abandoned. As darkness closed in over the grey seas, the Red Ensign and Foundation's flag blew out on the night wind. *Lillian* took station to leeward, and her people settled down to await the arrival of *Josephine*, and to hope for some moderation of the weather.

Josephine was bearing down toward the *Leicester* with every revolution Chief Gilmour could tease out of the diesels. Vibrating like a harp-string to the strain of her driving gear, she plunged on through the darkness.

On her bridge, Myalls stood watch over the radar, alert not only for the twin blips which would identify *Leicester* and *Lillian* but also for a single blip that might reveal the presence of *Zwarte Zee*. Wally knew, as did everyone concerned, that until a line had been made fast to *Leicester* she was still technically abandoned. At midnight Cowley called *Lillian* in code:

MY COURSE 151 DEGREES WILL STEAM FULL SPEED TO 0200 THEN IF YOU NOT IN SIGHT WILL DF YOU PLEASE HAVE RADIO OPERATOR ON WATCH AT THAT TIME HAVE NO KNOWLEDGE WHEREABOUTS COMPETING VESSEL SUGGEST YOU PRESERVE RADIO SILENCE CASE HE ALSO USING DF YOU HAVE DONE WELL

At 0015 hours on the morning of September 27th, one of the lookouts aboard *Lillian* spoke in a low voice. It was almost as if he feared to be overheard.

"Masthead light, bearing 315 degrees."

Crowe and all his officers clustered on the bridge, staring through their night glasses at the tiny distant light bearing down upon them from the northwest. Was it *Josephine?* Or was it the *Zwarte Zee?*

Crowe stepped into the wheelhouse, rang for half speed, and began edging *Lillian* in closer to the black bulk of *Leicester,* like a sheep dog placing himself close to the flank of a fat ewe as he scents the approaching wolf.

The wheelhouse was filled with the electric rustle of static from the loudspeaker of the radio-telephone, now turned on at full volume and tuned to the channel used by the Foundation tugs.

The moving star on the horizon brightened until the watchers could make out, through their binoculars, the dim glow of green and red navigation lights. The three lights formed a perfect triangle. The stranger, whoever she might be, was bearing down on a collision course for *Lillian.*

Then, with such abruptness that even the helmsman jumped, a metallic voice boomed into the confines of the wheelhouse.

"Got you on radar," it said, without preamble.

The voice was that of Wally Myalls.

Thirty-five minutes later the two tugs lay side by side, within hailing distance. After exchanging information through megaphones, *Josephine* switched on her searchlight and slowly circled *Leicester.* The derelict presented an eerie, almost spectral sight in the blaze of light, and *Josephine*'s people experienced the same sense of awe that *Lillian*'s crew had felt the previous evening.

After a time the glaring light went out and the tugs lay to, one on each side of the *Leicester,* in the heavy swell, their engines stopped, waiting for the dawn.

CHAPTER 2

Leicester's position was then about 800 miles from Bermuda and from St. John's, Newfoundland; 900 from Halifax; and 1100 from New York. These were the four ports from which Cowley, now in full command of the operation, had to select his ultimate destination.

He already knew Featherstone's opinion favouring Bermuda, but the decision remained in Cowley's hands. The dominating factor was the kind of weather he might anticipate en route to each of the four ports.

If he attempted to sail to Halifax or to St. John's he knew he must expect rough weather, since by the end of September the autumnal gales begin to dominate the northwestern approaches. On the other hand, if he sailed towards Bermuda he ran the risk of encountering another hurricane. Already 1948 had developed into one of the worst hurricane years in a generation and the season was not yet ended. New York, the final possibility, was ruled out by distance.

The choice seemed to lie between St. John's and Bermuda. Cowley decided to postpone his final decision until he had solved the immediate problems of getting a tow wire aboard the *Leicester* and then discovering whether she could be towed at all without causing her to turn on her beam ends and go down. Meanwhile Robbie Vatcher was instructed to obtain both the current and the long-range forecasts for the Bermuda and St. John's routes.

Vatcher immediately began to try to work New York, but there were a good many outgoing messages being transmitted and he had to wait. One of these was addressed to the *Zwarte Zee*.

INFORMATION FOUNDATION TUGS HAVE
CASUALTY CONSIDER NO PERCENTAGE

FURTHER EFFORT RETURN NEW YORK
TOW TANKER LENA BRODIN OSLO

Thus the shadow of *Zwarte Zee*, which had hung over the whole operation for so many days, was lifted.

By dawn on the 27th the weather had improved a little but it was still far from ideal. The risk of boarding remained extreme. Nevertheless, at 0600 hours *Josie*'s dory was shoved overside and four men jumped into it. They were Wally Myalls, Ray Squires, and Able Seamen Albert Greene and Thomas Farrell—Newfoundlanders all. Chief Diver and Salvage Foreman Squires remembers every detail:

"Our job was to try to get aboard on the forepart of the ship. While Wally figured out a way to hitch up the tow I was supposed to see whether the ship was in condition to be towed, and to decide if she'd stay afloat once strain came on her.

"Farrell rowed us over, and it was a scary sight. *Leicester* looked like she would roll right over on top of us any minute. None of us could swim and by now there must have been thirty or forty sharks hanging around to watch the show.

"When *Leicester* was coming down Farrell stuck the dory's stern practically right into one of the scupper holes, held it for about a second and then pulled out to sea. It was just long enough for Greene to jump. He landed in the scuppers in about four feet of water but when she rolled back up again he was still aboard.

"We stood off and watched him. It was comical. The decks were wet and covered with fuel oil, and slanting steeper than a toboggan run. When the ship rolled to starboard and eased the list, he'd manage to scramble a few feet up the deck. Then she'd roll back to port and shoot him down into the scuppers again. The sharks were just as interested as we were and once I thought a couple of them were going to go aboard and join him.

"We were laughing loud enough for him to hear and he turned and thumbed his nose at us. After about twenty minutes he got up far enough to catch a hanging rope-end and used it to get on the weather coaming of one of the hatches. After that it was no trick to reach the starboard rail. He hung on there until he could sling a rope down to the lee scuppers, and we started in again.

"This time Wally jumped—but Farrell was a wee bit slow pulling away and *Leicester* snagged the stern of the dory in a scupper hole and started to roll up with it. She lifted the dory right clear of the water before we slipped free and walloped back into the sea. The sharks looked awful disappointed when we stayed afloat.

"The third time in I made the jump, grabbed the rope and hauled myself up to the weather rail. Wally had already worked his way forward to the anchor winch and Greene had disappeared somewhere.

"First of all, I decided to go aft. It was easy walking along the weather alleyway, with one foot on the deck and the other on the cabin bulkheads. The whole alleyway looked like a rummage sale. Trousers, coats, shirts, socks, and every darn thing you could think of was strewn along it. There were even half a dozen sextants still in their boxes along with fifteen or twenty suitcases and seabags. I could see that *Leicester*'s crew had figured on travelling light when they abandoned ship.

"*Josephine* was getting pretty short of grub, and we had seen a vegetable locker on *Leicester*'s stern, so I headed for it. It was chock-full of spuds and stuff like that. But it didn't do us any good. Any man who could have carried a bag of spuds along that after deck, and lived, would have had to have two sets of wings.

"I gave up on the spuds and thought it was about time I went down into the holds and had a look around. Mind you, I wasn't all that anxious to go below. But it had to be done. There were small companion hatches between the holds and I pried the cover off one of them and started down the ladder into Number 3.

"It was pitch dark down there, and the ladder had such a list I couldn't use my feet. I went down like a monkey on a trapeze. I had a small flashlight and it was just bright enough to show me what had happened.

"The shifting boards had let go right the length of the hold, and two or three hundred tons of ballast had gone over against the port side of the ship. I guess it was the same in all the other holds but I never went to look. When I got out of Number 3 I was so glad to see the sky again I could even forgive Farrell for halfway drowning me.

"Wally came back along the weather rail to join me. He figured the only thing to do was to stop off the port anchor, burn through the port anchor chain, and attach our towing wire to it. It was going to be a big operation, on that deck, but we figured we could manage if we had a few more hands and some portable burning gear.

"We had to go back to *Josie* for the stuff. Before we went, Wally and I figured we should try and close the storm doors along the port alleyway because the water was still coming into the accommodations and running down to the engine room every time she rolled her lee rail under.

"We had quite a time of it. We'd slip along, knee deep in water, to the first door and then grab hold of the dogs and hang on while she rolled down. The whole alleyway would fill up and we'd be under water for a while, then she'd rise and we'd work like mad to get *that* door closed and the dogs pounded home. Then we'd watch our chance and make a dash for the next one. I kept expecting to find one of the sharks coming in to give us a hand, but I guess the look on Wally's face scared them off.

"When we got them all shut, and the water mostly out of our lungs, we began to wonder what had happened to Greene. I went back up to the weather side and all of a sudden I saw something coming along the starboard alleyway. For a couple of seconds my heart almost quit beating. Here was this figure working his way along toward me, dressed up in full officer's uniform, peaked cap and all, and carrying a sextant.

"He saw me too and up went his arm in a pretty smart salute. Then he grinned, and I recognized Greene. I don't put any stock in ghosts but he sure gave me one bad moment.

"Greene had come aboard in the scruffiest, worn-outest

clothes you ever saw, but he went back to *Josie* looking
like something off a training ship.

"Wally and I picked up the sextants and tied a pair to
each end of some neckties that were lying on the deck,
and slung them around our necks. Then we went down
to the lee side, sliding on our fannies and hanging on to
the rope. Getting back aboard the dory was worse than
leaving it, but we finally all got in and headed for *Josephine*."

Squires reported to Cowley that he thought *Leicester*
would remain afloat, even under tow, now that the accommodation doors were closed, providing she was towed
at a slow speed and not subjected to any more heavy
weather.

Myalls reported on how the towing wire ought to be
made fast. This was to be no simple operation. *Josephine*'s
towing wire was two-inch-diameter steel cable, and four
hundred feet of it weighed a ton. Normally a ship needing
to be towed has steam or electric power on her own forward winches; all that is required is to pass her a gradu-
ated series of lines, each one of increased diameter, until
the last one can be hauled aboard the casualty on her
winch and bring the towing cable with it.

Since there was no mechanical power aboard *Leicester*,
the connection had to be made by means of man power
alone. This is the way it was done.

The dory returned to *Leicester* carrying the original
four men plus Buck Dassylva—pumpman and general salvage genius—as well as a big iron snatchblock and a portable oxyacetylene cutting outfit.

The snatchblock, cutting gear, and gas cylinders were
hauled up the slanting deck and eased forward to the eyes
of the ship. Then two men unrove a length of wire from
Leicester's rigging and wove this back and forth through
a link of the port anchor chain, making the ends fast
to *Leicester*'s forward bitts. This was to secure the anchor
so that, when the chain was cut, it would not plunge
into the sea.

When the anchor was safely stopped off, Buck got busy
with his burning gear and severed the anchor chain.

Meanwhile another man had made the snatchblock fast. Now a snatchblock is simply a pulley set between two sheets of iron, one of which is hinged so that instead of having to insert an end of rope through the block you can lift the hinged section and lay the bight, or loop, around the pulley.

When all was ready, Wally stood in the bows and signalled to Cowley. Very gingerly Cowley backed the big tug toward the casualty's bows until less than fifty feet separated the two ships. Then a light heaving line was flung up to Wally from *Josie's* after deck. When this was hauled aboard *Leicester* it brought with it a manilla mooring line which was made fast to *Leicester's* bitts.

The two vessels were now tethered together and Cowley called Gilmour in the engine room and ordered the propeller to be kept barely turning over so that a gentle strain would be applied to the mooring line. This was to prevent *Leicester* from surging forward and plunging down on the tug's stern.

After this first step was completed, another heaving line was thrown aboard *Leicester* and the salvage crew hauled it in, bringing with it the bight of a three-inch manilla rope, both ends of which remained aboard *Josephine.* Dassylva slipped this bight into the snatchblock. One end of the three-inch rope aboard the *Josephine* was now made fast to a hundred-pound U-shackle on the end of the towing wire. The other end was passed around *Josephine's* electric capstan; and very carefully the shackle and towing wire were hauled aboard *Leicester.*

Even with the help of *Josie's* capstan it was all the men aboard *Leicester* could do to get the immense shackle and the heavy wire into position. When this was finally accomplished the free end of *Leicester's* anchor chain was shackled to the wire, and the connection was complete.

The next step was equally tricky. After passing out of the chain locker, the heavy anchor chain ran over the gypsy-end of *Leicester's* winch before terminating at the towing shackle. Now it was Myalls' job to ease off the winch brakes by hand and allow *Josephine* to haul about three hundred feet of chain out of the chain locker.

The mooring line was cast off and *Josephine* began to ease ahead, taking a strain upon the wire.

The chain paid out over the winch and through the port fairlead with an ugly roar. At the proper moment, Wally and Dassylva applied the brake, while at the same instant *Josephine* ceased pulling.

The winches alone could not take the full towing strain, so the chain had to be further secured aboard the *Leicester*. This was now done by inserting what is called a "devil's-claw" into one link of the chain, and by then weaving steel rope back and forth between the bitts, through several other links.

There were three reasons for using the anchor chain instead of making the towing wire fast directly to *Leicester*'s bitts. In the first place, the use of the winch and devil's-claw, together with the auxiliary wires to the bitts, provided a three-point anchorage for the towing wire— a matter of some moment since *Leicester* represented a ten-thousand-ton deadweight object. In the second place, a length of anchor chain included in the towing complex provides what salvage men refer to as a "spring." The great weight of the chain tends to sag the towing wire so that there is less likelihood of its being stretched to the breaking point under a sudden stress.

In the third place, the use of a chain passing over the casualty's bows greatly reduces the "sawing" or chafing effect, which can sever even a two-inch wire in a matter of hours.

While *Josephine*'s boarding party had been successfully completing the towing connection, a party from *Lillian* consisting of Higgins, Rose, and one helper had again boarded the *Leicester* in an attempt to free the jammed rudder so that when the tow began the ship would not tend to sheer off to one side of her course. Rose and Higgins descended into the very bowels of the ship to reach the rudder flat, but their efforts proved unavailing and the rudder remained jammed.

Though every man concerned had worked as though his

life depended on it, it was 1120 hours before the last of the boarding parties was clear of *Leicester* and Cowley could give the orders to begin the tow.

He had now decided on his destination. Vatcher had obtained a series of weather messages reporting the eastward movement of a low-pressure area down the St. Lawrence valley, with a consequent assurance of bad weather in the vicinity of Newfoundland. But to the south there were no signs of any tropical disturbances in the making and fair weather with light winds was predicted over Bermuda for the ensuing three days. The choice was obvious.

At 1123 Cowley rang for dead slow ahead. *Josephine* slowly gathered way. Wally Myalls, who was operating the enormous electric towing winch, paid out wire until the dial indicated that two thousand feet had left the reel. Then he carefully applied the brake, and the strain came on the wire.

It was a tense moment. At one end of the wire was ten thousand tons of dead ship; at the other, a 3200-horsepower tug applying a steadily increasing force. No one was worried that the wire might part—it was built to stand worse stress than this. But every man aboard both tugs was vitally concerned with the possibility that this heavy strain might be enough to alter *Leicester's* delicate equilibrium, and roll her over.

The wire passing over *Josephine's* stern began to draw bar-taut. The angle between the hanging anchor chain and *Leicester's* bows began to increase. Then, to the horror of everyone watching, the big ship rolled down farther than they had ever seen her go before; farther and farther, until the water was up to the lee coamings of her hatches.

In *Josephine's* engine room the telegraph swung to Full Astern; but even before the order could be obeyed *Leicester* began to recover herself. She came slowly back and the sea water streamed off her decks and ran home through the scuppers in a cataract of foam. *Leicester* was under way, moving almost imperceptibly. But she was under way.

At 1200 hours Vatcher transmitted the following message:

> MFML TO ALL SHIPS MFML TO ALL SHIPS
> AM IN POSITION 3510 NORTH 4640 WEST
> TOWING DERELICT LEICESTER 2000 FEET
> ASTERN WITH NO NAVIGATION LIGHTS ON
> TOW STOP COURSE 259 DEGREES SPEED
> THREE KNOTS VESSELS PLEASE KEEP
> CLEAR

CHAPTER 3

> FOUNDATION HALIFAX FROM MFML 1415
> AST 27 PROCEEDING ABOUT 4 KNOTS CASU-
> ALTY SHEERING BADLY UNABLE MOVE
> RUDDER STOP WILL BE CASE OF SLOW
> TOWING TO ARRIVE SAFELY STOP FOUN-
> DATION LILLIAN STANDING BY STOP EX-
> PECT WILL BE NECESSARY OBTAIN NAVAL
> AUTHORITIES PERMISSION ENTER BER-
> MUDA DUE DANGER GROUNDING CAPSIZ-
> ING IN CHANNEL STOP FIVE FEET WATER
> IN ENGINE ROOM NONE IN UPPER ACCOM-
> MODATIONS STOP K E E P I N G STRICT
> WATCH ON TOWING WIRE WINCH—COW-
> LEY

"She was a sight to make you think you were dreaming," Wally Myalls remembers. "With her rudder jammed hard a-port she was sheering off to port so sharp it looked like she'd decide to go to Florida instead of Bermuda. Sometimes she was nearly broadside to us, and then we'd have to slow *Josie* down to try and ease the *Leicester* back on course. When she was broadside like that the strain on the wire would pull her over so far her port boat deck would be just about submerged. If Squires hadn't got those accommodation doors dogged shut—" Wally Myalls is a modest man—"she'd have filled and sunk without a doubt.

"Cowley had a real problem. If he pulled too fast he'd be pretty sure to capsize her. But every hour we stayed at sea was one more hour for her to finish herself off. *Josephine* could have towed at eight or nine knots—we had the power—but while that rudder was jammed and she was sheering like she was, it would have killed her if we'd tried.

"I tell you, the boys watched that wire like a bunch of sealers watching for the first pan of whitecoats in the spring. Some of the salvage gang were always on watch, with a lighted burning torch beside them. They sat alongside the wire where it ran over the taffrail, and they never took their eyes off *Leicester*. If she'd started to plunge, they'd have had about a minute to cut the wire and let us get clear.

"Every change of watch we let out a few feet of wire and changed the position of the iron chafing plate that was bolted under the wire where it crossed the rail. That was to make sure the wire didn't chafe and break. We couldn't afford the time it would've taken to connect up again.

"You might have thought we'd have felt like celebrating—with that million-dollar boat behind us—but I tell you we were a pretty sober lot. Now that we had her at last the chance of losing her made everybody kind of sick. Bermuda was a long way off."

Bermuda was almost exactly 800 sea miles away when the tow began. At a towing speed of three or four knots, *Josephine* could not hope to bring her charge into a safe anchorage in much less than eight days—and that was too long. Following on the preceding period of gales, fair weather had come briefly to this section of the North Atlantic but no one but a wilful optimist could have expected the weather to remain amiable for eight more days. If the weather turned ugly once again, *Leicester*'s chances of survival under tow would fade away to nothing.

Cowley seldom left his bridge. Using every element of skill which the long years at sea had taught him, he nursed his charge along, always striving to move her just a little faster; but always aware that if he overdid it he would lose her by his own hand.

Lillian did what she could to help. During the day she kept station a little astern of *Leicester* and her people watched the big ship closely, ever alert to radio-phone a warning to Cowley if anything untoward developed. At night *Lillian* steamed abeam of the ship, and dangerously close to her, with her searchlight trained upon the derelict.

During the morning of the 28th, the wind dropped out to almost nothing for a few hours and the swells eased considerably. By noon Cowley had worked the tow up to a full six knots. At this speed *Leicester* tended to keep station almost abeam the tug's starboard quarter, without undue sheering. But at 1430 she suddenly seemed to go berserk. She sheered hard to port, bringing such a strain on the wire it was inconceivable that it would not burst. Cowley was forced to slow his tug down until she barely had steerageway; but still *Leicester* could not be persuaded to hold station. The struggle continued for three hours, and then for no apparent reason *Leicester* gave up the battle and returned to her old position off the starboard quarter.

During this day, the course of the tow followed a section of the great-circle track for low-powered steamers going to and from Gulf ports, and Cowley's Circus—which was what *Josephine*'s crew had named the tow—drew quite an audience. Four passing vessels altered course to take a closer look at the weird cortège making its way toward Bermuda. Vatcher was kept busy answering queries from incredulous onlookers—and Cowley was kept busy trying, by applied telepathy, to persuade the audience to stay to-hell-and-gone out of the way.

Seldom has any vessel been so avid for weather information as was *Josephine*. When Vatcher was not pestering the sore stations for the most recent prognostications, he was pestering every other ship within three hundred miles for minute details of the weather *they* were experiencing. *Josephine* came close to becoming a floating weather laboratory in her own right.

By midnight on the 28th, a northwest wind of Force 4 strength was blowing and the swell was getting heavier. Nevertheless the tow had made good nearly 180 miles during the 24-hour period.

In Halifax the onus of responsibility had passed from Featherstone to the Managing Director of Foundation Maritime, Edward Woollcombe. It was his task to conclude agreements and arrangements with *Leicester's* owners and, more vitally, with her insurance underwriters who had now come into legal possession of the ship. Before turning her over to her owners or to the underwriters Woollcombe was understandably anxious to ensure that his Company's rights would be safeguarded.

Negotiations were conducted by cable. Woollcombe's object was threefold; first, to establish the existence of a Lloyd's Open Form contract containing special clauses which took into consideration the vessel's total abandonment; second, to obtain definite financial commitments from the owners in advance of delivery to a safe port; and third, to persuade the underwriters and the owners that the safe port was to be the one of Foundation Maritime's own choosing.

The underwriters and the Federal Steam Navigation Company, on their side, were understandably reluctant to make any commitments until they knew their ship was safe. Furthermore, their concept of what constituted a safe harbour was one where *Leicester* would be secured from *all* further risks of loss. As far as Bermuda was concerned, this meant St. George's Harbour.

Woollcombe was just as anxious as anyone to see *Leicester* in a safe port. But careful calculations had shown him that *Leicester,* with a list of 50 degrees, would be drawing at least 26 feet of water, perhaps considerably more. The Admiralty charts of Bermuda showed the entrance channel to St. George's as only dredged to 27 feet. Moreover, the channel was barely 250 feet wide, and a tow as unwieldy and obstreperous as *Leicester* could be expected to sheer extravagantly enough to risk running ashore on one side or the other, if indeed she did not ground in the channel itself.

The alternative was Murray's Anchorage. This is an almost open roadstead lying at the northern tip of Bermuda, and protected from the sea only by an area of submerged coral reefs. Nevertheless in normal weather it was considered safe enough to be used by units of the British fleet, as well as by many merchant ships. And the channel leading to it was 38 feet deep and nearly 600 feet wide.

Woollcombe was also afraid that any attempt to bring *Leicester* into St. George's (even if such an attempt were feasible) would be met with stiff resistance from the harbour authorities who would be aware of the dangers of having the big ship turn turtle or go aground and thus deny the harbour to all other traffic. If the authorities proved recalcitrant the tugs and their charge might have to stay outside for hours, or even days; and every additional hour *Leicester* remained in deep water was an hour during which she might be irretrievably lost.

On the other hand, once she was moored in Murray's Anchorage, she would be in calm and shallow water and immediate steps could be taken to begin reducing her dangerous list to a point where she could safely enter St. George's.

Woollcombe was a past master of persuasion. After three days of suave, yet pointed, messages to London, he convinced his opponents that *Leicester* was already as good as saved, and he got his way, and a draft agreement. Its highlights were as follows:

1: The services are to be considered as rendered under the Lloyd's Open Form Salvage Agreement with appropriate additions to the contract whereby the owners agree that the vessel was abandoned and derelict when found by Foundation tugs.

2: The contract is to be considered successfully terminated when *Leicester* is brought to safe anchorage or moorage in Bermuda; it being agreed that *either* Murray's Anchorage or St. George's Harbour is to be considered as safe anchorage.

3: The owners agree to take full possession of, and he entirely responsible for the *Leicester* immediately upon successful termination of the above contract.

Now the rest was up to Cowley and the tugs.

Not many men aboard the tugs shared Woollcombe's calm assurance of a successful outcome to the tow. But neither were they overly pessimistic. In salvage work the game is never won until the job is done, and salvage men have a generally phlegmatic attitude toward the work in hand.

Their general phlegm was sorely tried late on the afternoon of September 30th. Up to this time the weather had remained reasonably benevolent, though always somewhat threatening. Cowley had gradually worked *Josephine*'s speed up, a revolution at a time, until the tug was towing at a full six knots, and occasionally approaching seven. By 1730 hours on the 30th, Bermuda lay only a little more than 400 miles away.

It was at this juncture that Chief Gilmour appeared upon the bridge. He was apologetic, but firm.

"The port engine's got a bad leak in the lubrication system, Captain. I'm going to have to stop the engine; and I can't even begin to guess how long it'll be out of action— not until we strip the lube system down and have a look."

Ten minutes later the engine was stopped. The tow dropped back to a speed of barely four knots and those aboard *Josephine* were not cheered by a fall in the barometer, or by the evening weather report which predicted southwest winds rising to Force 5 or 6 the following morning . . . head winds for *Josephine* and *Leicester*.

For a time Cowley considered turning the tow over to *Lillian* but even with two engines *Lillian* could not have moved *Leicester* much faster than *Josephine* was able to do with one. In any event, *Lillian*'s engines were now so overtired that Higgins was momentarily expecting either or both of them to break down. So *Josephine* retained the tow.

Down in the engine room, Gilmour's "black gang" worked like a bunch of navvies. They stripped the lubricating system down and checked it section by section.

But it was not until midnight that they found the leak. It had resulted from a broken casting in a circulating pump —and there was no spare pump available.

Fortunately *Josephine* was equipped with a small machine shop designed to manufacture parts which might be needed in salvage work. Equally fortunately, she had two first-rate machinists aboard. After working for three hours, these men machined a substitute for the cracked casting. By 0630 hours on the morning of October 1st, the lubrication system had been reassembled.

At 0641 hours the port engine started up and the shaft revolution counter began to climb again.

Things were not yet plain sailing. Gilmour, coming back again to the bridge in an almost unrecognizable state from oil, dirt, and fatigue, reported that he had lost over a thousand gallons of detergent lubricating oil, and would be forced to substitute straight mineral oil in order to keep the engines going. He did not know, and could not tell, what the result of this substitution would be, but he suspected it might well end in a totally seized and useless engine.

There was no alternative but to take the risk.

For once the weather prediction turned out to have been overly pessimistic. During daylight hours of October 1st, the wind remained light although it did swing into the southwest. The seas were moderate and *Leicester* towed well enough—considering. Cowley made use of this continuing period of grace to work *Josephine* up to a full seven knots.

By noon next day *Josephine* was within 160 miles of Bermuda, and Cowley dispatched a message to Featherstone in Halifax:

SPEED SEVEN KNOTS CASUALTY SHEERING EASILY ADJUSTING SPEED TO ARRIVE TOMORROW MORNING ASSUME YOU CONSIDER ADVISABLE DELIVER MURRAYS ANCHORAGE

Featherstone was not in Halifax to receive this message. He was air-borne at a point not far from Bermuda and, late in the afternoon of October 2nd, he was in St. George busily preparing for the reception of Foundation's million-dollar tow.

PART EIGHT

Featherstone liked doing things in a hurry. His first port of call was the Harbour Master's office. This amiable gentleman soon found himself being hustled into a hired motor boat and accompanying Featherstone out past St. Catherine's Head so that the Salvage Master could take a speculative look at the entrance channel to Murray's Anchorage.

Featherstone looked, grunted a few times, and made some notations in the ten-cent notebook he always carried with him. Once back at the landing stage, the Harbour Master found himself unceremoniously abandoned.

Featherstone then visited the offices of Foundation's local agents. Pandemonium followed for half an hour, at the end of which time arrangements had been made for two United States Army tugs and a British Admiralty tug to stand by at Five Fathom Hole—the Pilot Station—as of 700 hours the following morning. In addition, a gang of stevedores had been hired to begin shifting *Leicester*'s ballast as soon as she was moored, and all arangements had been concluded—some of them amicably—with the port and naval authorities.

Featherstone's next stop was at the home of the Chief Pilot. Here he called a battle council at which the pilots and the skippers of the local tugs received their campaign instructions. They were all a little numb by the time Featherstone departed for his hotel; but they knew exactly what was expected of them the following morning.

The Salvage Master was not entirely happy about the prospects for the morning. He was well aware of the difficulties of manoeuvring a dead ship through a narrow channel, particularly when that ship was listing 50 degrees and had her rudder locked hard to port. Even more disturbing was the risk that, if *Leicester* touched bottom, the narrow margin of positive buoyancy left to her would be destroyed, and the event that the seas and gales had failed to bring about would come to pass.

The mental picture of *Leicester* capsized in the centre of the busy ship channel was one to bring a shudder even to such a hardened old campaigner as Featherstone.

To complete Featherstone's day, a message was delivered to his room just as he was about to pack himself into bed for a few hours' sleep.

> US LIBERTY OSCAR CHAPPELL LOST PRO-
> PELLER 3600 NORTH 2535 WEST WE HAVE
> UNDERTAKEN TOW HER UNITED STATES
> STOP EXPEDITE DEPARTURE TUG SOON-
> EST LEAVE CHOICE TO YOU—WOOLL-
> COMBE

The disabled *Chappell* was about 2000 miles east of Bermuda. Brave man that he was, Featherstone dreaded the moment when he would have to tell either Cowley or Crowe to refuel in a hurry and get under way again.

The morning of October 3rd broke overcast with a gentle northwest wind to tickle the great ocean swells and wrinkle their long backs. A two-seater private plane took off from Bermuda airport into the whitening dawn and headed easterly with the cameraman for an American press service stuffed uncomfortably into the back seat.

As the little aircraft swung over Five Fathom Hole, the pilot could see two minuscule tugs lying motionless below him while a third was coming up from the southwest. But these were not the tugs the passenger was looking for. The plane climbed a little and headed out to sea.

Minutes later the pilot picked out three dark specks on the horizon. He waved his hand to warn the passenger, and went into a shallow dive.

As the plane left the island behind it, the pilot boat was putting out from St. George's. Featherstone, standing beside the wheelsman, might well have passed for some

fearsome figurehead on a buccaneering ship of long ago
... except for his cigar.

Aboard *Josephine*, Cowley stood on the bridge wing
and raised his binoculars. There, dead ahead, was the blue
loom of land. As the light strengthened he could make out
the white gleam of buildings in St. George and the brood-
ing hulk of Sugar Loaf Hill. Then his attention was distracted by the nasal roar of a small aircraft diving over
Josephine.

"Reception committee," remarked Wally Myalls. His
round face gleamed happily. The end of the long ordeal
of men and ships was now in view.

At exactly 0800 hours the way began to come off *Josephine*
and her crew began to shorten up the tow line. As the
little convoy closed with the land, the three harbour
tugs, their sirens sounding, came bustling out from the
entrance of the narrows. Leading them was the pilot boat
bearing an easily recognizable Featherstone who was so
far forgetting his dignity as to wave both hands high in
the air.

It was a magnificent moment even for the most blasé
members of the rescue tugs; but they had little enough
time to savour it.

The pilot boat bumped against *Josephine*'s bulwarks
just long enough for a pilot to leap aboard, then it was
off to *Leicester*. The pause here was a little longer, for
Featherstone and the Chief Pilot both had to be landed
on the derelict. Within minutes they had clambered up
the canted deck using the same ropes that had been fixed
in place by the salvage men at sea.

The pilot went directly to the bridge and wedged himself on the high starboard wing. Featherstone made a
rapid tour of the ship to satisfy himself that all was as he
had expected it to be, and that his plans would not be
upset by some previously unknown factor. Only then did
he join the pilot and give the signal for the tow to carry
on.

By this time *Josephine* had shortened up so that there
was less than three hundred yards of wire between her

and *Leicester*. The Army tug ST-10 had placed a hawser on *Leicester*'s stern and was falling back into a position from which she could help to steer the unwieldy hulk. The Admiralty tug *Justice* had come alongside on the starboard quarter and was ready to assist. *Lillian* and the second Army tug were standing by.

At 1005 *Josephine* passed between the two buoys marking the entrance to the channel. At that exact moment *Leicester* took a sharp sheer to starboard.

Cowley immediately put the tug's helm hard over; but *Leicester*'s sheer only grew worse. ST-10 began going full astern but *Leicester* still moved implacably toward the coral reefs which now lay less than a hundred feet away. *Justice*'s Master, sensing the urgency of the moment, did not wait for orders. He cast off his lines and slid his tug forward along *Leicester*'s exposed bottom until she could put her nose against the big ship's starboard bow. Then *Justice*'s crew began to kick the shallowing water into foam.

Slowly, slowly, *Leicester*'s bow began to swing back into the channel, back behind *Josephine*.

With the tow straightened out once more, Cowley discovered he was having trouble keeping *Leicester* moving. Baffled, he called on Gilmour for more power, but the big ship astern continued to hang back as if she were wilfully dragging her heels.

Featherstone and the pilot, glancing astern from *Leicester*'s bridge, saw the clear blue waters going milky white! *Leicester* indeed was dragging her heels, or rather her stern, upon the coral bottom.

There was nothing to be done about it. There was no room to turn in order to head her back to deeper water. The only hope was to continue towing and pray she was only running over a small area of spoil which the dredges had somehow neglected to remove.

At every instant Featherstone expected her to take the ground solidly. If that happened, he was convinced she would have rolled right over.

The entrance channel to Murray's Anchorage is two miles long. It took the combined flotilla of tugs just under two hours to ease the *Leicester*, still sheering erratically, still dragging her stern, through those two miles of torment. She was intractible to the last. As Myalls said afterwards, "That was the longest part of the whole damn tow."

But at 1340 hours *Leicester* cleared the inside channel approach, and *Josephine* swung her down the broad South Channel.

At 1406 hours *Leicester* lay securely moored to a battleship mooring buoy in Murray's Anchorage.

Lying quietly to the huge mooring buoy she was soon almost completely surrounded by a milling mob of small craft, ranging from luxury cruisers loaded with wealthy tourists, through dowdy harbour craft filled with staid officials, down to leaky punts rowed by laughing dark-skinned children.

On shore several hundred people lined the cliffs overlooking the anchorage and stared in wonder at the bizarre spectacle of this ship which seemed to be defying the laws of gravity and equilibrium.

Above the boats and the crowd a helicopter from the United States air base joined several light aircraft which were vying with one another to put their photographer-passengers into the best positions to get even more spectacular pictures of the *Leicester*.

As seen from the air, the ship resembled a grotesque sea monster whose unresisting bulk was being devoured by legions of carrion crabs.

First aboard had been the salvage gang. Several boat-loads of port authorities had followed closely after. Then came a delegation from the British Ministry of Transport, which had been flown from London to conduct a first-hand examination of the ship. These men were charged with discovering not only the causes of the *Leicester's* disaster, but also with determining once and for all the probable causes for the loss of so many of her sister ships.

There was also a boatload of underwriters and Lloyd's surveyors. There was a covey of agents and of owners' representatives, and there were innumerable boatloads of less readily identifiable local officials who had contrived some excuse, no matter how spurious, in order to board this Seven-Day-Wonder-of-the-Seas.

This gathering crowd, sliding and slithering over the hapless vessel, brought no joy to the hearts of the watching crews of the two salvage tugs which were now anchored a few hundred yards away. Since the search began, the tugboat crews had imperceptibly come to feel that *Leicester* was their personal property. Now they began to experience a mounting resentment at the manner in which *Leicester* was being overrun by strangers who had taken no part in the odyssey of her rescue.

Aboard the ship, Featherstone was in the thick of the invasion, and he was soon steaming mad. The owners' representatives had boarded *Leicester* shortly after she moored. When Featherstone gave them a smiling greeting and prepared to hand over their ship to them, he was met by glum expressions and by a lack of cooperation which he took for the rankest kind of ingratitude, if not stupidity.

"Sorry, Captain," one of them said. "We can't take the responsibility of accepting delivery out here. We'll have no part of her until you put her into St. George's Harbour."

Featherstone kept his temper while he explained that the Lloyd's Open Form contract, duly ratified in London, specified safe delivery of the ship *either* to St. George's or to Murray's Anchorage. This did no good and the owners' representatives remained adamant. St. George's it had to be or they refused to claim their vessel.

"Now look!" said Featherstone, whose face was turning lobster-red, "this ship has been rescued on the high seas *by our people*. Without us she'd have gone down. We've done all we contracted to, and plenty more, and now she's safe. She won't stay safe unless you take over pretty smart and get on with the job of putting her back in trim. She's not going to balance there on her side forever while you fellows wring your hands and chatter about St. George's Harbour. I've already arranged for a stevedoring gang to start shifting ballast. I've got pumps standing by on *Josephine* ready to put on board. But the contract says she's *your* ship, and so I can't do another thing until you tell me to. Now what about it?"

Nothing about it, was the uncompromising attitude of the owners' representatives. They were playing it very safe. While any risk of losing the ship remained, they wanted no part of her.

Meanwhile the Ministry of Transport inspectors and the underwriters' investigators had removed the hatch coverings from Number 4 hold and had begun to crawl about amongst the maze of shattered shifting boards and bent stanchions, and over the piles of sand and gravel, in the 'tweendecks space.

It had, of course, been apparent from the first that the disaster to the ship had been caused by the ballast shifting. What was not apparent was how the shift could have occurred in the presence of the shifting boards. It took some hours of digging, prying, and peering before this mystery was solved.

The answer turned out to be painfully simple. The 1500 tons of ballast stowed 'tweendecks had brought such a weight to bear upon the lower deck that it had sagged at least three inches. Since the upper, or weather, deck had remained in position, the effect of the sag had been to tear away the fastenings on the bottoms of the upright stanchions which held the shifting boards in place. Because the bottoms of these stanchions were buried out of sight under six feet of ballast, there was no sign of their dislocation which *Leicester*'s people could have detected. However, when *Leicester* took her heavy roll during the night of September 14th–15th the whole complex of boards and stanchions had swung out, like a top-hinged gate, allowing the ballast to go thundering down to the low side.

The concept of fitting shifting boards had been sound enough. The error had lain in the failure to anticipate the effect of a new stress added to the innumerable stresses to which a ship is subject. This failure had very nearly cost her life, and had in fact cost the lives of six of her men.

It was an error which would not be repeated—thanks largely to the successful efforts of the Foundation tugs. In saving *Leicester,* so she could be examined by experts, the tugs in all likelihood had been the salvation of other *Sam*-class ships which would not now be subjected to the once-mysterious doom which had overwhelmed so many of their sisters in the past.

While *Josephine* lay anchored off *Leicester,* forced to stand by until the handover could be completed, *Lillian* sailed into St. George's to take on supplies for the voyage back to Halifax.

Her people were in a merry mood. Five days would see them home at last with each man getting a healthy bonus cheque as a reward for his part in the *Leicester* job.

First Mate Jimmy Rose was on the jetty supervising the fueling when Featherstone arrived by taxi. The Salvage Master was benign, polite, and even ingratiating as he asked Rose where the Skipper was. Naturally, Rose immediately felt a sense of apprehension.

Twenty minutes later Crowe was telling him the news. *Lillian* would sail at dawn the following morning—*for a point a hundred miles to the eastward of the Azores,* where the Liberty ship *Oscar Chappell* was drifting helpless. "And then," Crowe said, "instead of dropping her off at Horta and making a beeline for home, we have to drag her right the way back across three thousand miles of ocean to New York!"

Rose made no comment. He could think of nothing really adequate to say. But his silence was more than made good by *Lillian*'s crew. Higgins managed some brand-new descriptive phrases. As he assured Crowe, *Lillian*'s engines were not only tired, they were practically worn out. "I hope," he muttered darkly as he left the Captain's cabin, "every damn one of you knows how to row a boat!"

As the afternoon waned, the mood of *Josephine*'s crew continued to be tinged with a growing dissatisfaction. When they heard that *Leicester*'s representatives had refused to accept the ship, and that *Josephine* would therefore have to lie anchored alongside her all night, with no shore leave being granted to anyone, their resentment grew.

"I tell ye, Byes," said one of the deckhands who were grouped on *Josie*'s after deck, moodily staring at the lights flicking on upon the shore, "they'uns had their chance to take her. If they don't want her, we'uns better keep onto her."

When, an hour later, *Josephine*'s motor boat departed shoreward carrying Captain Cowley with some of the other officers and even Freddie, the ship's dog, the departure was watched by many disapproving eyes.

An hour after dusk two of the Newfoundlanders stood together at *Josie*'s rail, morosely eyeing the black hulk of the nearby *Leicester*. Suddenly one of them (and no one can quite remember which it was) was smitten with an idea of such brilliance that he was hardly able to express it.

"Ye know, Bye," he said when he had straightened out his words, "'twouldn't be so hard to put a heaving line aboard that boat . . ."

It took a moment for the idea to sink in. When it did, the second sailor brightened considerably. Expertly he estimated the distance between *Josephine* and *Leicester*. It was not more than a hundred feet. The night was still, the waters were dead calm.

Ten minutes later a desilent group assembled on the

deck. In the hands of one man was a large meathook filched from the ship's refrigerator, and attached to it was a neatly coiled length of heaving line.

There came the swish of a hard-flung object . . . followed by a splash.

"Never mind, me son," someone whispered hoarsely. "Give her another heave."

This time the swish was followed by a muffled clank. Gingerly the dark figures took a strain upon their end of the heaving line. Something clattered across *Leicester's* deck, then the line came taut.

"Got her, by God! Careful now, me sons, this un'll be the biggest squid you ever jigged. Pull aisy now!"

They say that a fly can exert sufficient pressure to move the *Queen Mary* if that pressure is applied long enough. This may or may not be so. But it is an indisputable fact that two men pulling very gently on a quarter-inch heaving line can swing the stern of even such a big tug as *Foundation Josephine*.

Her stern kissed *Leicester's* side so softly that there was hardly a sound. Within seconds two mooring hawsers that just happened to be handy were slipped across to the the big ship and made fast.

"And that," says the anonymous memorialist of the events which followed, "was the moment when we began to catch the pirate fever.

"It didn't hit us all at once, you understand. First off just two of the lads went over to the *Leicester*. There she lay, dark and ghostly and not a light showing on her anywhere. Some of us didn't feel too keen to go exploring through her insides at night, particularly when we remembered the men she'd lost.

"The two fellows still hadn't come back when Wally Myalls turned up on deck. With the skipper ashore. Wally was in charge. He didn't need to be told what was going on. 'Cast off those lines, you bunch of pirates,' he says. 'We can't,' we answers. 'There's two of us already gone aboard.'

"Wally thought about that a minute, then he turned to Farrell and Green.

" 'Go over there and bring them two back, and do it quick. If the Old Man catches you aboard the *Leicester* you'll be logged from here to Christmas.'

"So those two goes, and the rest of us and Wally waits. And waits. *Nobody* comes back. Wally was getting mad. He picks two more, and tells them if *they* don't show up in ten minutes bringing the others with them, he'll put the whole lot in the jug ashore.

"Well, they never come back neither. So this time Wally sends one of the junior mates and one of the engineers. And damned if *they* didn't disappear. By now pretty near half the crew had gone and Wally was getting desperate. He didn't dare lose any more men, and he didn't dare go aboard himself because he knew every man-dick of us would jump ship about ten paces behind him.

"Just about then there was a kind of shout from *Leicester,* and somebody came shooting down the deck and into the rail. We picked him up. It was the customs officer that had been left on board to guard the wreck. He was a pretty nervous man.

" 'Listen,' he says to us 'that ship's not healthy! There's things movin' about all over her. You fellows let me come over on your boat. I'm not staying on her no longer!'

" 'Goddam it!' Wally says to him. 'Them ain't "things," them's Newfoundlanders! You stay right here and don't you let a man-jack go over to that ship. I'm going to round the rest of them up before they strip her clean!'

"With that Wally jumps the gap and disappears. A minute later the customs man takes a look about him and finds he's all alone. By that time I was halfway up *Leicester*'s deck myself, but I could hear him down there, hollering like mad for us not to leave him. I don't think he cared that we were aboard the *Leicester.* I think he was just all-fired lonely.

"In a way I don't blame him for the way he felt. *Leicester* may have been a 'dead' ship, but right about then she was the liveliest dead ship you ever saw. There must have been twenty men on the prowl and every one of them was trying to keep out of the way of all the others. In the accommodations and the passageways it was black-

er than a whore's heart, and pretty near nobody had
flashlights. Those that had 'em were trying not to use 'em.
Once in a while a match would flare up and you'd get a
glimpse of a face and a couple of shining eyes, then it
would all go black again.

"Pirate fever is the queerest thing. It isn't *what* you take
that counts; it's the fun of taking it. I was feeling my way
along the passage to the Master's cabin when I fell right
over some fellow who was crawling along the other way
on hands and knees. I lit a match to see what was what,
and there was someone I knew with a pillowcase slung
over his back for a bag, and it jammed to the top with
rolls of toilet paper.

"The longer we stayed aboard, the worse the fever got.
Someone would get hold of something he wanted, like a
radio, and cache it in a secret place and then go looking
for more loot. When he came back for the radio someone
else would have swiped it from *him*. Chances were it
would be lifted from the second fellow too, and before
the fun was over probably everybody aboard the boat
would have had their hands on that radio at least once.

"I fell in with a chum of mine and we kept together. It
seemed cosier that way. By then the ship was filled with
queer noises—whispers coming out of ventilators, scuf-
fling sounds, clanks and bangs. I shone my light into one
cabin and there was one of the engine-room gang sitting
on that sloping floor pretty near surrounded by shoes. He'd
found a fit for the right foot but darned if he could find
its mate, in the dark. He had about a dozen neckties strung
around his neck too, and he had a bottle in one hand that
he'd been swigging at. I was kind of sorry we turned the
light on him because then he could read the label, and
that may have spoiled his fun a little. It was a pint bottle
of Cascara.

"It's a wonder someone didn't get drowned, or killed.
Some of the fellows would be walking along passageways
when they'd come to a companionway they couldn't see,
and the next thing they'd be going down it head first. No
one knew where anyone else, including himself, had got
to. And all you could do was keep on feeling your way

along until eventually you got back out on deck. One chap fell down the engine-room ladder into five feet of water and had to swim for his life. He set up a holler, and it was a good thing for the customs officer he never heard *that* voice wailing up out of the bottom of the ship, or he'd have jumped overboard for sure.

"Some of the chaps were more practical than others. One of them brought seventeen suits back aboard the *Josie*. He'd go over to *Leicester* wearing nothing at all and keep putting on suits, one on top of the other, until he could just barely waddle. He'd stagger over to the tug; then he'd go back for another load.

"Somebody else found the ship's safe and was all set to go and get the burning gear. But he got interested in a souvenir music box he stumbled over in the dark, and that satisfied him.

"I just happened to be back on the *Josie* when I heard the motor boat coming and knew it was the Skipper. He came aboard and asked for Wally, and I told him Wally was over on the ship.

"'Well,' he said, 'but where's the rest of the crew? I want to move to a new anchorage.'

"I told him I didn't know where they were; but by this time he could see the black figures flitting down the *Leicester's* deck, with pillowcases slung over their backs. He let a yell out of him, and then damned if *he* didn't hop aboard the *Leicester*. I suppose he was just trying to get some of the crew back on board, but he sure took a long time about it.

"By about midnight the fever had begun to die down and after another hour everybody was back aboard the *Josie*. Cowley never said a word, but in the morning he sent the Mate to tell us the door to the Salvage Master's cabin would be left open, and that at noon it would be closed, locked and sealed. He didn't need to say another thing. The fever was all out of us by then. All morning you'd meet fellows heading for the Salvage Master's room with big bulges under their jackets or their shirts.

"Nobody minded that the stuff all had to go back. We'd had our fun."

October 4th began badly for Featherstone. *Leicester*'s representatives still refused to accept delivery of their ship and the Salvage Master's impassioned cable to Woollcombe in Halifax had not yet resulted in any action which would break the impasse.

Featherstone had other worries too. He had decided that, for the safety of the ship, he could not tolerate any further delay in beginning the task of uprighting her. At 0800 hours he had gone to the office of his own Company's agents to arrange for the dispatch of the stevedoring gang, only to discover that the stevedores appeared to have dissolved into thin air. The agent apologetically mumbled something about a shortage of labour, but it was soon apparent that the real reason for the disappearance of the stevedores was their unwillingness to board a ship which, apart from the fact that she might turn over at any moment, was now believed to be haunted by the phantoms of her lost crew members.

The stories related by the customs man after his return to St. George at dawn that morning must have lost nothing in the telling.

Drastic situations require drastic remedies—an old saw which had always been one of Featherstone's favourites. By 0900 hours he had managed to bring a local magistrate to such an acute realization of the merit and urgency of his cause that a work gang of prisoners was released from the local jail.

These unhappy fellows were ferried out to the ship and promptly put to work 'tweendecks in Numbers 4 and 5 holds.

Featherstone had early recognized that the task of restoring the ship to a safe trim was going to be no easy one. Due to the extreme list of the vessel, clam buckets lowered into the holds could not reach most of the material which had to be removed. Therefore every pound of ballast in the port 'tweendecks spaces had to be shovelled up by hand, carried to the hatch openings, and there dumped into buckets which were lowered down from *Josephine*'s after derrick boom. When these buckets had been laboriously filled they were run up, swung overboard and dumped; but considering the many hundreds of tons of flinty gravel and sand which would have to be removed before the ship could begin to right herself, Featherstone was soon casting about for other ways of reducing the list. He devised two expedients.

A motor-driven two-inch pump had been lowered into *Leicester*'s flooded engine room and lashed securely to the slanted gratings. Instead of running the discharge pipe up to the deck, and overboard, Featherstone ordered it run to the ship's starboard void tanks so that pumping would serve the double purpose of freeing the engine room and at the same time of adding weight to the high, starboard, side of the vessel.

The second expedient was to put a gang into the *lower* hold of Number 5, right on the bottom of the ship, and to set these men to work shifting about a hundred tons of ballast over the shaft tunnel (which acted as a dam running the full length of Number 5) to the starboard side of the hold.

Once the work was well under way, Featherstone returned ashore to dispatch *Lillian* on her five-thousand-mile journey to the Azores and back. *Lillian* duly departed at 1430 hours; but there was no gay dockside ceremony, no cheerfully waving bunting, and no showers of prettily coloured strips of paper. *Lillian* went glumly, without a word, without a single farewell blast of her whistle. She went, as one of her people remarked, "just like one of them old-time Frenchies heading for the guillotine."

There was at least a ray of happiness for Featherstone

PART NINE

Leicester's owners might not have been so ready to re-linquish their advantage had they been able to see the hurricane map in the Washington office of the United States Weather Bureau.

This map, which had been wiped clean of markings after the death of Hurricane VIII somewhere at sea off Flemish Cap on September 26th, now bore a significant new network of notations.

Centring on a point 150 miles to the east of British Honduras was a spreading pattern of concentric circles which looked very much as if someone had flung a gigantic rock into the Caribbean Sea and had then photographed the resultant ripple pattern. Each of these concentric circles represented a line connecting many points of equal barometric pressure; and each succeeding circle (working inward toward the centre) marked a decrease in pressure of one-tenth of an inch. In the very middle of this complex was the familiar *L*, to mark a major low.

Beside this *L* was the blue-pencilled numeral IX.

This ninth hurricane of the 1948 season appears to have been born during the night of October 2nd-3rd, only a few miles off Cape Gracias a Dios on the coast of Nicaragua. Like its immediate predecessor, it at first appeared to be a rather mild manifestation of the Serpent's Coil, doomed to an early death by the presence of a massive and overriding Continental High which was sagging southward over the Gulf of Mexico. But Hurricane IX possessed a much greater vitality than the weather observers at first realized.

During the 12-hour period from 2000 hours October 3rd to 0800 hours October 4th, this cyclone took form and substance with such effect that an unfortunate fruit ship that was enmeshed in its coils reported herself as being totally disabled in winds of 100 knots and in seas running thirty feet in height. When her report reached Washington, the hurricane experts at the Weather Bureau knew they had the makings of another monster on their hands.

Oddly enough, no general hurricane warning for any portion of the North Atlantic was issued that day. Perhaps the hurricane experts were still not sure of ix's survival. Perhaps they did not yet have enough information on which to base a prediction as to its future actions.

However, by dawn on October 5th they had information in abundance, at least as to the potency of the new cyclone.

During the night the Serpent's Coil reached and encompassed the northwestern tip of Cuba. Though the centre passed well to the west of Havana proper, the damage done in Cuba's capital—where wind speeds of 132 miles per hour were reported—was catastrophic.

In two hours' time thirty-four vessels were sunk in Havana harbour. During the same two hours an additional fifteen schooners and small coast freighters were either sunk or driven ashore at Batabanó. Damage to buildings and crops in Pinar del Rio province alone was believed to run as high as twelve million dollars.

What was even more significant to the weather experts was the fact that the Continental High, covering tens of thousands of square miles with its massive mountain of air, appeared to be retreating in the face of the fury of the approaching hurricane. It began to appear that Hurricane ix would not only strike at the United States, but might then proceed north and northeast along roughly the same ocean track which had been followed by Hurricanes vii and viii.

By midday of the 5th, the cyclone's centre was almost over Miami Airport, having destroyed or badly damaged 700 houses, and sent more than 21,000 people into emergency Red Cross shelters. By 2100 hours the centre began passing out to sea near Fort Lauderdale.

In Murray's Anchorage, Featherstone had been driving his working crews to the limits of their endurance in order to get the *Leicester* righted quickly. On the 5th, in order to speed things up, he chartered a floating crane and had her brought to the *Leicester* where she was employed removing ballast from the forward holds.

During the late afternoon a boisterous easterly wind began to blow and within an hour it had kicked up such a chop in the shallow exposed waters of the anchorage that it was no longer possible to keep either *Josephine* or the crane alongside the ship.

Although forced to stop all work for the remainder of the day, Featherstone felt tolerably content with the progress made so far. *Leicester*'s list had been reduced to 36 degrees, so there was no longer any real risk of her capsizing. All the same he was anxious to right her another fifteen or twenty degrees as quickly as possible so she would be fit to be towed into the fully protected waters of St. George's Harbour. With luck, and better weather on the morrow, Featherstone expected to be ready to move her by October 7th.

When the last work gang left *Leicester* on the afternoon of the 5th, Featherstone accompanied them ashore. He went immediately to the weather office to ask how long the easterly blow was expected to continue. It was then he first heard about Hurricane ix.

This new hurricane was of only academic interest to the Bermuda weather men, since its course had now been predicted by the United States Weather Bureau to follow a northwesterly track which would clear Bermuda by several hundred miles.

As to the local blow, the meteorologists were able to assure Featherstone that it would die down by the morning of the 6th—and he went off to his hotel content with this.

Featherstone may have been irritated by the arrival of the easterly storm but *Josephine*'s crew were delighted by it. For them it meant the first chance to get ashore since arriving at Bermuda, and they were in a mood to make the most of the opportunity.

One of the St. George's harbour pilots, a jovial dark-skinned fellow who had become friendly with some of *Josephine*'s crew, volunteered his motor boat as a water taxi. Scrubbed, shaven, and dressed in their best shore-going rig, the men piled into the launch, already reasonably merry. Within an hour they were becoming unreasonably merry. The Sommers Inn, the St. George Hotel, the White Horse, and half a dozen other ports of call were soon aware that they had been invaded by travellers from the cold and foggy island to the north. Being Newfoundlanders, most of the men had begun to develop a taste for good red rum shortly after they were weaned, and to find themselves in this land where rum ran like water seemed rather like a foretaste of paradise.

"We had one old chap from Come-by-Chance," remembers Vatcher, "who had been at sea with the fishing fleet since he was seven, and who was pushing sixty when he came on the *Josephine*. In all that time he had never had his fill of rum. Just after we got ashore, a local laddie came up to him and offered him a quart bottle of blackstrap for fifty cents. Old William looked at the bottle and then at me as if he thought he must be already drunk. It was just too good to be believed. He had to pay his half dollar and drink the bottle on the spot before he figured it was true.

"I happened to be coming out of the White Horse a couple of hours later when I ran into him again. He had picked up a wheelbarrow somewhere and it was full up, right to the top, with bottles of black rum. Old William was hiking her right along for the docks, singing 'The Kelligrew Soirée' at the top of his voice. When he sees me, he gives a whoop. 'Stay where you're to, Sparkie!' he yells, 'till I gits this lot in a dory. Two more loads and we can sail for Come-by-Chance and never have to put to sea again!"

Not all the voyagers were as single-minded as old William. Several of them, of Irish stock and from the Southern Shore, decided to engage in the Irishman's favourite pastime and they began fighting their way from pub to pub. As they roared down one dark street they met a coloured policeman who stopped them.

"We are very hospitable here in Bermuda, gentlemen," the policeman explained courteously. "We do not really mind if you kill each *other*. But I must remind you it is against the law to kill a member of the local citizenry."

Nor was love forgotten. It is no man's place to recall in public the amorous adventures of his friends; but it is impossible to refrain from mentioning one incident which magnificently confirms the legendary prowess attributed to all true Newfoundlanders.

After having spent an hour drinking with his companions, one of the smaller of the crew members decided he had wasted enough of the evening. He was seen to set sail from the vicinity of the Sommers Inn convoying no less than seven lolloping women, any one of whom looked capable of eating him in two good bites.

But when the motor boat was ready to make its precarious return passage out to the *Josephine* in the small hours of the morning, this man amongst men arrived back at the dock *carrying over his shoulder* a 200-pound lady of the night. When someone asked him what he intended to do with his squirming baggage, he replied happily, "Well, Bye, the Skipper he's got a dog aboard, so I figure he won't kick if I brings along a bitch."

It had been, withal, a reasonably good night. The following day was not so good.

Shortly after the prison gang returned to work on the morning of October 6th, they began to show signs of mutiny. When they were asked the trouble, one of them explained that they "could smell death down heah" in Number 4 'tweendeck space. One of the mates went down to test the air, and confirmed that there was indeed a rank, putrescent stench. The prisoners had concluded that the odour came from a corpse—perhaps one of the missing members of *Leicester*'s crew. Having thought about this for a time, they resolutely refused to continue work.

This left Featherstone with only one alternative. Shamelessly he dragooned the crew of the *Josephine* into picking up shovels and pitching into the remaining mass of ballast in the blistering hot, stinking holds of *Leicester*. Those of the crew who had glimpsed heaven the night before were now convinced they had sunk straight back to hell.

During the afternoon the vessel's list was reduced to 26 degrees. Featherstone considered that another night's work would make her ready for the tow into St. George's and he tentatively scheduled this tow to begin at noon on October 7th.

His plans were upset when a strong southwest wind began to blow during the late afternoon. Combined with a rough sea this again made it impossible for the crane or for *Josephine* to remain alongside. Reluctantly, the Salvage Master had to discontinue operations for the night.

After putting out to sea late on the evening of October 5th, Hurricane IX had set its course almost due northeast. Shipping in the danger area had been warned, and the Serpent's Coil found nothing to assault except the seas themselves. By 2000 hours on the 6th it had travelled almost 500 miles along its predicted course, and any potential threat it might have posed to Bermuda seemed to have faded into insignificance. The prediction issued at midnight on the 6th indicated that the centre would be passing 200 miles to the westward of Bermuda shortly after noon on the 7th. No warning was issued at Bermuda and no special precautions were taken, not even at the big American base near St. George.

The morning of the 7th broke clear, with a moderate southwest wind still kicking up something of a sea in Murray's Anchorage. but not enough to interfere seriously with work on *Leicester*.

Shortly before noon the shovel of a man digging in Number 4 sank into something soft. There ensued a gruesome few minutes until further excavation revealed the corpse of an extremely defunct dog. One of the oldest and least savoury sea-going jokes in the world had been perpetrated upon *Leicester* by the shore gang at Tilbury when they stowed the ballast. The dog was now belatedly consigned to a watery grave, and work went on until it was time to knock off for the noon meal.

It was a humid and oppressive day, and after he had had his lunch Vatcher lay down on his bunk and prepared to have a snooze. He was not yet asleep when the cabin door opened and one of the mates stuck his head into the room.

"You awake, Sparkie? There's a blinker light pointed our way from the signal station. It's too fast for me—can't read it; but I got our call sign a couple of times."

Vatcher sat up reluctantly. "Okay," he said. "I'll switch on and give 'em a call."

He sat down in the swivel chair in front of the panel, switched on transmitter and receiver and tuned the set to 2182 kilocycles, the standard calling frequency for voice transmissions. Then he picked up the microphone.

"*Foundation Josephine* calling Bermuda Radio, *Foundation Josephine* calling Bermuda Radio. Do you have a message for me? Over."

Static and the whine of a carrier wave beat back through the loudspeaker, and then was overlaid by a crisp British voice.

"*Foundation Josephine*, this is Bermuda Radio. Range Two."

Vatcher twirled the frequency dials to Range Two—2134 kilocycles—and drawing a message pad toward him, prepared to write.

"*Foundation Josephine*, this is Bermuda Radio. Here is a special weather report. West Indian hurricane reported three hundred miles southeast Cape Hatteras at 1000 AST moving northeasterly at eighteen knots. Hurricane winds covering an area of eighty miles circumference and gale winds extending one hundred miles from centre. Strong southerly to northwesterly winds expected at Bermuda during this afternoon and evening . . ." there was a pause, and then the voice continued in a much less official tone: "You'd better put an extra anchor on that whale you've got out there. Wouldn't want her going back to sea again. Over."

"Bermuda Radio—*Josephine*," Vatcher replied. "Thanks for the tip. We'll tie her to your radio mast. Over and out."

Cowley read this message without much visible concern.

"Wally," he said to his First Mate, "check the moorings on *Leicester* and double them up if you think it best. Looks like we might have a little dust-up later on. And get someone to take this weather report to Feathers, will you?"

Featherstone got the message a few minutes later. Walking carefully down *Leicester*'s deck, which was now canted less than 20 degrees, he jumped across to *Josephine*'s bulwarks and made his way to the tug's bridge. He went directly to the barometer, tapped it, and stared at the needle for a long moment. There had been a fall of two-tenths of an inch during the past six hours—and this was a warning which could not be lightly disregarded.

Cowley came quietly into the chart room and said:

"You've noticed the fall too? It doesn't look all that good. I think we might get more than the weather boys expect."

Featherstone took a long look through the chart-room window at the western sky, which was already blurring and hazing as high streamers of white cloud spread over it, and at the distant surf booming heavily against the outlying coral reefs. Then his gaze moved to the dial of the anemometer which was showing a southwest wind at 25 miles per hour.

"We may get more than *anyone* expects," he said abruptly. "Best batten down for trouble."

Fifteen minutes later the crane had left *Leicester*'s side in tow of a diesel-powered workboat Featherstone had hired two days earlier. The working gang, including a group of prisoners who had been persuaded to return after the discovery of the dead dog had allayed their fears somewhat, continued shifting ballast to the starboard side of various holds while they awaited the return of the workboat which would take them to St. George's.

Several members of *Josephine*'s crew were set to work doubling *Leicester*'s mooring to the battleship buoy. The original mooring had consisted of *Leicester*'s own anchor chain shackled to the ring on the buoy. Now this was backed by a length of two-inch-diameter wire cable.

The rest of *Josephine*'s crew were busy doubling the moorings between the tug and *Leicester*. By the time they finished, the two ships were almost literally knitted together by a complex of wire ropes and eight-inch manilla hawsers. When that was done, the whole crew turned-to battening *Josephine* down to ride out a heavy blow.

Aboard *Leicester*, the salvage gang was occupied at similar tasks—replacing the boards and covers over the open hatches, and closing off all ports and doors.

Shortly after 1400 hours a flight of four patrol bombers had taken off en route for Tampa, Florida, on a routine training mission. The big aircraft had gone thundering into the air only a few hundred yards above *Leicester* and her attendant tug.

Barely twenty minutes later the flight leader had begun calling his Bermuda base, and what he had to report was of a nature calculated to send the base meteorologists into an immediate flurry of activity. The results of this activity were relayed by telephone to Bermuda Radio, and at 1452 hours the station was transmitting in both code and voice.

Vatcher, who had been ordered by Cowley to remain on listening watch, was almost deafened when the international code began to clatter out of his loudspeaker over 500 kilocycles:

BERMUDA RADIO TO ALL STATIONS EMER-
GENCY HURRICANE WARNING WEST IN-
DIES HURRICANE CHANGED COURSE
EASTWARD HEADING DIRECT BERMUDA
ETA BETWEEN 1900 AND 2200 HOURS TAKE
IMMEDIATE PRECAUTIONS

Except for the masters of the several vessels lying in Bermuda waters—men who could smell approaching weather without the aid of radio reports—the sudden change in the course of the hurricane caught the islanders off guard. Even after the emergency warning was broadcast, there were many who thought it was probably a false alarm.

They had some reason for their doubts. In order to threaten the island directly, Hurricane IX would have had to alter its course by nearly 40 degrees, and do so within a matter of an hour or two. It was not really credible that this could have happened.

But it had.

"It was almost as if the damned thing suddenly took a look around from fifteen thousand feet and saw Bermuda off to the east, with the *Leicester* lying there in Murray's Anchorage. If it had been human, or inhuman but sentient, it could hardly have reacted more directly. One minute it was heading into the northeast. The next, it spotted the ship which two previous hurricanes had failed to sink, and it seemed to make up its mind right off the bat, deciding it would finish off the job." This from a meteorologist. This from a scientist—and scientists are not much given to anthropomorphic explanations of natural phenomena.

The patrol aircraft encountered the forefront of the cyclone about 75 miles from the island. Though the pilots could readily determine that it had changed course, they had no way of ascertaining the speed at which it was moving. Thus the prediction of the arrival time of the hurricane at Bermuda was necessarily based on the speed last reported for it—18 knots. In fact, having turned toward its chosen victim, Hurricane IX was now roaring in from the west at more than 35 knots—an almost unheard-of speed for West Indian cyclones in this latitude.

Some of the island dwellers may have failed to take sufficient notice of the radio warnings; but the masters of the ships lying in Murray's Anchorage did not make the same mistake. They had been keeping a weather eye on their own barometers all morning and, having noted a drop of a tenth of an inch between 1400 and 1430, most of them had already given stand-by orders to their engine rooms even before the emergency message was broadcast. By 1510, every ship but two in Murray's Anchorage was either under way or was hurriedly bringing its anchors home.

The Anchorage was no place to be caught by a hurricane. In those constricted, reef-studded waters, totally unprotected from north, west or southwest winds, and very slightly protected from really heavy seas, a ship's master who chose to remain in so dubious a shelter was pushing his luck to the limit. The alternative, and the only one, assuming that it was impossible to find mooring in St. George's, was to put to sea, get well clear of the reefs, and then steam in such a manner as to keep the body of the island between the ship and the prevailing direction of the hurricane.

Standing on *Leicester*'s bridge, the Salvage Master watched a cruiser, three destroyers and six merchant vessels, all of which had been peacefully at anchor half an hour earlier, steaming at full speed toward the exit channel. It was not a sight to engender a feeling of complacency. Nevertheless there was nothing Featherstone could do which he had not already done to protect the *Leicester*. She could not be moved towards St George's Harbour—the hurricane would certainly catch her on the way. She could not be towed out to sea for, even if there was sufficient time for this manoeuvre, she would stand little chance of weathering the blow outside. All she could do was stay "where she was at," as the Newfoundlanders put it, and trust to her doubled moorings and to the three ten-ton concrete anchors of the battleship buoy.

But this was not *quite* all. She could, if Featherstone and Cowley so decided, also put her trust in *Josephine*.

At 1520, as the motor launch was bucking its way back out to *Leicester* through an increasingly heavy chop, Featherstone boarded *Josephine* and spoke to Cowley.

"The choice is yours, John," he said. "*Josephine* is your vessel and I can't give you orders where her safety's at stake. If you think you ought to go to sea, I'll support you. But if you think it's a reasonable risk to stay alongside, I'll support that too. Frankly, I'd hate to see you go. I'd feel we were abandoning this ship. The power you've got might make the difference whether she rides this one out or whether she goes ashore. If we leave her and she breaks free and drives out to the reefs, that's the end of her. If you stay, and the same thing happens, it might be the end of *Josie* too. But it would have to be one hell of a hurricane to shift the two of you, with those concrete anchors down and your thirty-two-hundred horsepower to ease the strain."

Cowley did not hesitate. He had already thought the matter through and he agreed with Featherstone that it would be little short of cowardice to abandon *Leicester*— even though she was not their vessel, nor even their responsibility now that the L.O.F. contract had been fulfilled.

"We'll stick it out, Cap," he said. "We'll ride it out."

By the time Featherstone regained *Leicester*'s deck, the motor launch was back alongside. She looked as if she had had a rough trip of it for her "captain" and "engineer" were both busy bailing and pumping, while five of *Josie*'s crew stood by with boathooks to keep her from staving her gunwales in against the tug.

During the preceding half-hour both sea and wind had risen so rapidly that they were now of full storm proportions. Seaward, the swells preceding the hurricane were bursting over the barrier reefs with a roar which could be heard seven miles away in St. George, and with a violence that sent the spray leaping fifty feet into the darkening air.

To the westward the sky had assumed the terrible black mantle of the hurricane bar. Air pressure was dropping so rapidly that no mechanical barometer was needed to indicate the fact—every man was his own barometer, as human organs, sensitized by apprehension, registered the decrease physically. Storm scud was already sweeping in, almost at masthead height, and only a cold grey light filtered vaguely through the rolling cirrus clouds above.

The local labourers aboard *Leicester* were clamouring to get ashore. They did not need to be warned of what was coming. All their lives they had known hurricanes, and they were acutely aware of the risks *Leicester* would run when the great wind struck. Featherstone was equally anxious to get them and a party of marine surveyers off the ship. He had no desire to risk anyone's life unnecessarily; but by now it had become a toss-up whether it might not be safer for them to remain aboard than to risk a passage through the gale-swept anchorage in the little motor launch.

He had already concluded that it was too dangerous to risk the journey when, with freakish suddenness, the wind fell light. The labourers at once set up a furious demand to be taken off; and in this they were joined, though more sedately, by the surveyers. However, the surveyers did not trust the boatman's ability to keep his little launch afloat in the seas which were then running. The skipper of the boat was inclined to agree with his detractors, for he was a harbour man and by no means used to facing heavy weather in the open.

Torn between the fear of staying and the fear of going, the group of passengers—numbering twenty-five in all—were wasting precious time. The lull could not last long and after it the hurricane would strike.

Featherstone made up his mind in a hurry.

"I'm going to take them in," he shouted up to Cowley on *Josephine*'s bridge. "I'll try to get back out to join you."

Cowley waved a hand in acknowledgement, but already Featherstone had leapt aboard the launch. Soon she was turning in the lee of the *Leicester* to make her dash for land.

As she came out of the lee into the full-fledged storm seas, Featherstone took station beside the wheelsman and quietly ordered him when to let the boat fall off, when to hold her up, and how to weather the bigger seas.

Before they had gone a mile the wind began to rise again and backed into the northwest, driving straight toward the shore. Almost at once the white surf began to boil along the edges of the seaward cliffs.

Featherstone brought the boat in until she was on the very edge of the surf.

"There was a three-to-five chance she would fill at any minute. If she did, all we could do would be to put her straight into the surf and hope she'd hold together until the seas had thrown her on shore. That way we would have saved most of the passengers. If I'd kept her too far off the shore and she'd swamped, damned few of them would have stayed alive.

"The passengers were all jumbled together down in the pit forward, and when we got in close enough so they could hear the surf thundering like the drums of hell, they didn't seem too happy. Every second or third sea was coming aboard us, and they already looked half drowned.

"The boat was just a little thing, never meant for anything but harbour work, and she didn't like that sea at all. She had a sort of imitation funnel over her diesel and every now and then a big one would break over us and part of it would go straight down onto the engine. Thank God it was a diesel. A gas engine would have quit after the first drenching. The diesel kept on going, though it sputtered enough at times to make me think we were for the surf.

"There was a bunch of the pilots on Sugar Loaf Hill—they'd come out there to see what we were going to do about *Leicester*, I guess—and I could see them waving their arms and trying to get us to risk running the boat ashore. That was a chance I was prepared to take, but not until I had to. I kept my eye on the shoreline pretty close, watching for beaches or strips of shingle. I had in mind a little cove near Tobacco Bay where there was some shelter, and I figured if we got that far, we could beach her safely.

"St. Catherine's Point lay just beyond Tobacco Bay and when we got opposite the bay I thought we might just make it right around. The boat was half full of water, but everyone was bailing and she seemed to be good for another couple of hundred yards. That was all we needed, so I held on, and sure enough we rounded the Point and got into the lee of the land beyond. Half an hour later we were in St. George's. By that time the boat had about three inches of free board left, and the passengers were sitting to their waists in their own private bathtub."

There was of course no question of Featherstone's attempting to get back aboard the *Leicester*. During the passage in, the wind had risen to Force 10. Accompanied by torrential rain it had whipped the entire Anchorage into a boiling broth of foam and milky seas. The Salvage Master was ashore for good.

Aboard the two vessels lying in the Anchorage, things were going well enough. *Leicester* was lying head-to-wind and showing no signs of dragging. The moorings between the two ships were under great strain but were holding well. Cowley and his crew concluded that things were not likely to get much worse and they were now fully confident that both ships would ride out the blow. Some of the men even went below to wash and shave, and to prepare for a late evening ashore after the hurricane had blown itself out.

The instruments at the Air Force base had registered gusts of 80 miles an hour, and the barometer indicated that the eye of the storm had almost arrived over the island. Since the winds in the forward quadrants of any cyclone are usually stronger than those in the rear quadrants, it was to be assumed that Hurricane ix had already displayed its utmost ferocity.

At 1830 the wind veered to southeast and began to fall light. By 1845 a flat calm lay over Bermuda. The black storm scud began to thin, and patches of blue sky showed overhead. The island was now in the eye.

There was a general release from tension. People who had sought shelter in basements or in hurricane-proof buildings began to reappear on the streets. Those who from the start had not been inclined to take Hurricane ix seriously were now smugly self-satisfied at their own prescience. It looked as if the worst was over.

Having made his way to the St. George Hotel, Featherstone ordered dinner. While he waited for it, he joined the group in the hotel bar, and he was in a relaxed and amiable mood when his ear caught a sound which the other guests did not yet hear. It was a distant low-keyed moaning; rather felt than heard. Featherstone stiffened. In five paces he had gained the lobby door and was staring into the western sky.

He could not see much, but he could see enough. The whole western vista had gone black, not with an absence of colour and light, but with a solid and overwhelming weight of what might as well have been black basalt rock. It was as if a mountain had suddenly turned fluid and was rolling in upon some insignificant piece of flotsam.

All down the street the shadow of an approaching cataclysm ran at the heels of people who were fleeing in search of whatever shelter they could find. Featherstone shouted the alarm through the hotel, and staff and management alike rushed to close the storm shutters and barricade the building against the imminent assault. The guests were herded into the central lobby and storm lanterns were brought out from their ready storage places.

The moaning had risen in key and was becoming an all-pervasive sound, a stomach-chilling vibration. The world went dark and the flicker of lightning flame in the approaching coil of the serpent did not illuminate: it only intensified the horror of the spectacle.

Featherstone and the hotel staff knew what was coming. Most of the guests did not. Many were tourists from the mainland and some were actually entertained by the preparations which were going on around them. They found it most exciting.

Aboard *Josephine* no one was entertained. The people of the salvage tug were, unabashedly, afraid. They had an uninterrupted view of the approaching nemesis and most of them were only too well aware that it might prove to be their nemesis in very truth.

Nevertheless they remained calm, almost detached. They had donned the same strange armour which infantry soldiers adopt during the last minutes before they come under the annihilating impact of an enemy barrage.

Freddie Squires and Wally Myalls moved unhurriedly along the decks, making a final check to see that everything was snugly battened down. Cowley joined them and personally examined all the moorings. Nobody glanced up at the swelling coil which was about to embrace them and the world about them. They knew it was there. They were in its shadow; and the darkness poured in upon them like warm treacle.

At 1900 hours the second half of the hurricane struck Bermuda. Within three minutes the wind was gusting at 122 miles an hour. Within ten it had blown away every anemometer on the island.

The rain began—though it was unlike anything we think of when we use the word. It drove parallel to the ground and with such power that it shredded the shore vegetation almost as thoroughly as an immense shotgun blast might have done. Where it struck human flesh, it made deep pockmarks which could still be seen a week after the hurricane had passed.

In the lobby of the St. George Hotel the electric lights flared once and died. The storm lanterns cast a flickering and sickly glow. The hotel shook with the tremulous agony of an old and dying man. The roar of the hurricane had become so all-encompassing that the human ear and mind could no longer accept it. It was as though every person in the lobby had suddenly been stricken deaf.

It was a dying time; and to some of those who experienced the grip of the Serpent's Coil that night of October 7th, it seemed that this *was* death.

It was also no time; for the passage of the minutes bore

no relation to the movements of the clocks upon the walls. Yet, by the clocks, it was three hours later before individual guests realized that they could hear again.

Voices that had been dumb were raised anew. People began to laugh—and some to weep. The walls of the hotel still trembled, but not with the agony of death.

At that moment there came a thunderous knock upon the barricaded lobby door.

"It even startled me a little," Featherstone remembers. "We knew damn well there ought to be no living person on the streets. Nobody moved for a minute; then the manager went to the door, raised the bars and, bracing himself against the wind, swung it back a little. Someone dressed entirely in black oilskins, and glistening like an eel just out of the ocean, squeezed past him and the two of them jammed the door shut again and barred it.

"The stranger came forward a bit so we could see him in the light of the lanterns, and when he took off his sou'-wester I recognized Ray Squires at once."

CHAPTER 5

Before the eye of the storm began passing over Bermuda, the cyclone had been blowing from southeast. After the passage of the eye, the raging winds which again burst upon the island did so from the northwest.

When the period of calm began, *Leicester* and *Josephine* were lying bow to bow, facing into the southeast. Consequently when the terrible wind heralding the arrival of the second portion of the hurricane struck, it caught the two vessels from astern.

In any ordinary gale they would have swung in a semicircle with the battleship mooring as a pivot, and would have again presented their bows to the wind. This was no ordinary gale.

"When that unholy terror slammed into us, it was like we'd been rammed by an icebreaker coming up from astern. We never had a chance to swing. The wind pushed us forward right over the battleship mooring.

"I was in *Josie*'s wheelhouse and I could see the buoy—it was a steel drum about twenty feet long and maybe ten in diameter—slide off *Leicester*'s port bow and come down between her and *Josephine*. I could guess what was going to happen when it wedged in between our bow and *Leicester*. As I watched the damn thing, I was so interested I never even opened my mouth. Not that words could have helped us then.

"The buoy fetched up between the two ships with a jolt that nearly shook me off my feet. By the time I got a grip on something and peered out again, I couldn't see the buoy or anything.

"It wasn't the rain coming down that cut visibility to zero, it was the ocean going up. The first gust of wind blew away the hurricane seas as if they'd been made of sawdust. It blew them right into the air and turned them into a kind of salty muck that was too thick to breathe, and too thin to swim in. There wasn't any boundary between sea and air; you couldn't tell where one began and where the other quit.

"We might just as well have been in a submarine for all we could tell of what was happening around us. We couldn't see anything, and the roar of the storm was so bad we couldn't hear anything. It was like living in a silent movie. Cowley, the Squires boys and three or four others were all in the wheelhouse, and we could see each other's lips moving but you could hardly hear a word unless you stuck your ear right up against the other fellow's mouth.

"We didn't need to hear or see, to know what that buoy was doing. It was jammed between the two ships like a wedge, and both ships were driving down on it as if they were under full power in the open sea. They told us afterwards the wind was supposed to have reached speeds of more than 140 miles an hour—and a wind like that can do some pushing!

"The worst of it was, the buoy had dragged the mooring chain right under *Leicester*'s bottom so she couldn't swing and get her head around into the wind. She was caught almost broadside-to, and not even thirty tons of concrete anchors could have held her broadside against that blow for long.

"Something had to give. Cowley figured the only hope for *Leicester* was for us to let go our lines so the buoy would free itself and let the *Leicester* come round head into it. He rang the engine room for stand-by and then Wally and a couple of deckhands undertook to go out on deck and cast off the lines.

"They had to crawl on hands and knees, and they damn near suffocated. The wind was so strong you could hardly suck the air into your lungs—and when you did the wind would suck it right back out. Anyway, the stuff you got wasn't air at all—it was salt-water soup.

"Wally reached the starboard forward bitts somehow

though, and he saw right away it was impossible to do anything with the lines, except maybe cut them. The tension on them was so great nothing could have slacked them off.

"Our bow mooring was a doubled length of one-and-a-quarter-inch towing wire—the kind old *Foundation Franklin* used to have on her winch, and plenty strong enough to haul a big ship through a winter gale. It was made fast to the bitts or niggerheads, which were of heavy cast iron and bolted right through the deck into the ship's frames. The wire was crossed around them both.

"Wally could only see about five or six feet in front of him—what with the muck that was flying about. He was lying there trying to figure what to do next when he noticed the bitts *start to bend in toward each other.* He didn't believe his eyes at first, but when he looked along the wire to where it went through the bulwarks, he saw that the fairlead—that's an iron casting two inches thick —had broken like a piece of glass and the wire was cutting its way back through the bulwarks.

"He had to wiggle some to get out of the way. By the time he got back to the accommodations, that wire had cut through thirty feet of half-inch steel plating as easy as opening a sardine can. Then the forward bitts snapped off. We never heard them go but we felt the ship give a heavy shudder, and we knew.

"After the bow mooring went, the rest didn't take long to follow. There were steel wires and eight-inch ropes bursting like bits of string all down our starboard side, until we were only held by a single ten-inch manilla hawser aft. Someone crawled out on deck to try to cut this with an axe, but before he got to it we had swung right around and smashed our port side against the *Leicester*'s bow, buckling half a dozen shell plates on *Josie* and making a hell of a dint in the *Leicester* as well.

"Then the ten-inch line parted, and we were free.

"Cowley rang for full speed on both engines. We knew we had just one chance—and that was to get *Josie* headed up into the wind and hold her there with the engines. There wasn't much room to play about in either. There were coral reefs on three sides, and the land on the fourth.

"*Josie* had thirty-two hundred horsepower—more than there is in some ocean liners. But even with both engines going at full revs she still wouldn't come up into that wind! She couldn't do it. She kept blowing sideways; and only God knew where she was blowing to.

"Dave Clark was at the wheel—as good a wheelsman as you'd ever find—and he tried every trick he knew to make her head into it—and got nowhere at all. Things were getting right desperate about then, so Cowley sent Wally forward to let go the anchor—we just had one anchor left, we'd lost our second hook on the *Orion* job. Wally crawled out there again, knocked off the brake, and let run about seven shots of chain. The hook caught, and we could feel just a little bit of a jerk and then the chain parted like it was made of mud.

"It was just twenty-five minutes since the wind first hit us, but I tell you it seemed like twenty-five hours. When the anchor chain broke and we knew we were teetotally out of luck, every minute got as long as a year.

"The wind hadn't let up one bit. Every now and again a real nasty gust would take us on the quarter and lay us right over—the way a man would kick over a beer bottle with his foot.

"We were all straining our ears to catch the roar of breakers on the reefs, but we might as well have tried to hear a tin whistle in the middle of a fiddlers' contest.

"Things weren't so good down below either. We'd taken a lot of damage when we hit the *Leicester* and the pumps were working hard to keep the water down. God only knows what Gilmour and his crowd thought was happening up on deck. If there was any prayerful men amongst them, they must have been working overtime to get a hearing.

"Freddie—the skipper's dog—was in the wheelhouse with us, and I felt real sorry for him. He was getting too old for this sort of stuff. All he wanted to do was find a quiet corner and lay down. But every time he got settled someone would fall over him, or a sea or gust would hit us and heel us over, and he'd go sliding across the deck.

"By this time we all had our life preservers on and we were just standing by—or holding on as you might say—waiting for her to hit. It was going to happen, and nothing on God's green earth could stop it.

"Cowley had told Vatcher to send an sos, though what good that was going to do I couldn't figure. Maybe it was so if we went down all-standing, someone would have a hint of what had happened. But Vatcher wasn't having any luck with his radio. His aerials had blown away and, as we heard later, even the big steel transmitter towers on the island had blown down too, so he couldn't have talked to the shore stations anyhow.

"The wind had shifted some, but it wasn't steady in any quarter, and we didn't know how far or in what direction we had drifted. There was a chance we might have been blown through the entrance channel, but there was a damned sight better chance we were already in among the reefs.

"We'd been out there banging around like a bird in a paper bag for just twenty-seven minutes when there was a hell of a bump and the old girl keeled over on her side. She straightened up again all right, but from then on it was just one bump after another; like a baby falling down the stairs. Between rolling, bumping and pitching, you couldn't keep your feet at all.

"Cowley grabbed the phone and tried to get the engine room, and luckily Chandler was on the other end trying to get Cowley. They howled at each other for a couple of seconds, and then Cowley turns to us and hollers that she's filling fast.

"The boys in the engine room just made it up the ladder one jump ahead of the water. Some of them weren't quite fast enough. It was already up to Gilmour's knees before he reached the top rung. Three minutes after we'd hit, *Josie* was a stone-dead ship—no power, no lights, no nothing.

"When *Josie* struck, Ray Squires and Buck Dassylva had been down in the salvage hold checking to see that the gear hadn't started to break loose. The lights went out and there they were in the pitch dark, with the ship sinking under them. Instead of making for the deck, they went all around down there closing the watertight doors, and doing it by feel.

"*Josie* was still moving. Each big sea that lifted her would shove her over a new reef and she'd come down on the coral with a God-almighty jolt.

"A few of us tried to get down to our cabins to rescue some personal belongings, but by this time most of the accommodations were flooded. Vatcher got into his room, which was about half full of water since *Josie* was listing about thirty degrees to starboard by this time, and damned if he didn't find one of the oilers in there with a sick cat. They were both too sick to move. Vatcher had to carry the cat, and kick the oiler, all the way to the saloon.

"Then the saloon started to fill with water so we all crowded into the wheelhouse where Cowley and Wally were trying to decide what the chances were of launching a boat. Four of us went to work on the door to the boat deck, and we could just barely hold it from blowing right off its hinges when we opened it. Cowley went out, with Freddie Squires right behind him, to see what could be done.

"Between them they got the starboard boat cut loose— but they never got to launch it. The wind caught it, and it lifted right off the deck and went flying into the night. After that there didn't seem to be any point in fiddling with the port boat.

"The list wasn't getting any worse, so we figured we were probably hung up on the edge of a reef and being held there by the pressure of the wind. What worried us was the chance *Josie* was on one of the outer reefs and might slide off into deep water any minute. If that had happened, she'd have gone down like a stone.

"It was night time now, but that couldn't have made it any darker than it had been before. The air didn't just look black, it *was* black. You could have cut chunks out of it and made a fortune selling the stuff to funeral parlours. The hurricane still wasn't letting up one damn bit. We didn't know if we were glad, or mad, about that. If it didn't let up we'd never know where the hell we were, or have a chance to get away. But if it *did* let up, *Josie* might slip into deep water and take us with her. No man, even with a lifejacket, was going to live more than ten seconds in that sea.

"*Josie* struck at 1945 hours, but it wasn't until nearly 2200 hours that the hurricane began to abate. As soon as we could, we pried open the door to the port wing of the bridge and we carted all our flares and signals out there and started to touch them off. It was a dandy fireworks show. Trouble was, no one ever saw it. The spray and rain was still so thick you couldn't have seen Cape Race Lighthouse if it had been fifty feet away.

"As the wind began to fall out, Cowley thought we ought to have another try at launching a boat; but the port boat was too high up now and we couldn't swing her over —which was probably just as well. Vatcher got busy and cut the Carley Float loose and a couple of the hands were just going to grab hold of it when zip, it got airborne too. Nobody ever did see hide nor hair of it again.

"Vatcher watched it go, and then he says to me: 'By God, if I get out of this I'm going to sea no more!' There weren't many fellows aboard *Josie* right about then who would have give him any argument.

"Buck Dassylva was prowling around on the port side with a boat-hook, and he kept poking it down into the foam alongside. Nothing ever bothered Buck. He was singing at the top of his lungs:

"'No CAN Do . . . No CAN Do . . . Nobody NOHOW NO CAN Do!'

"All of a sudden he stops singing and gives a bellow. The wind was falling fast by now and the sea water that had gone up into the air was dripping back where it belonged, so you could see a little better. Some of us went over beside Buck and we could just make out something looming up hard on the port quarter.

"'By Gar, I tink dat's land!' says Buck. And sure enough it was.

"An hour later the sky was clear, and the wind was hardly strong enough to sail a dory in. It was what they call a beautiful tropic night. You'd have thought the whole thing had been some kind of rubby-dub's night-mare. Right alongside us was a little island. We shoved the gangplank over to it and everybody walked ashore with dry feet, just as comfortable as if they'd been coming off a P. & O. liner at Southampton.

The island was joined to the mainland by a narrow neck, and somebody recognized the place. We'd gone ashore on Ferry Point at the south side of Whalebone Bay, not half a mile from where *Josie* and *Leicester* had been moored! So we knew where *we* were, but there wasn't a thing to be seen of *Leicester*.

"Before the hurricane died out, Cowley sent Ray ashore to hoof it cross country to St. George and tell Feathers what had happened. Then he got the rest of the crew settled down in an abandoned gun position on the little island. Later on we salvaged some blankets and the odd mattress out of the wreck, and we brought the bonded liquor supply ashore so it wouldn't get damaged.

"After a while, when we were settled down a bit, Buck starts pacing to and fro.

"'Wat the matter weeth you fellows, heh? Everybody get dressed and shave to go ashore tonight. Now you *got* ashore all you want to do is sleep! By Gar, I never see such a lazy bunch. I guess I go to town alone!'

"And be damned if he didn't too."

Except for Buck Dassylva, doggedly enjoying his night ashore, *Josephine*'s crew tried to get some rest. Vatcher, bunking on a sodden mattress laid upon the coral, woke to discover that the mattress seemed to be heeling over on its beam ends and was apparently pitching and heaving in a desperate fashion. To his dismay he discovered that the mattress would not lie still even when he was fully awake. Only when he gripped its edges with both hands and hung on to it for several minutes did it capitulate. As a delayed reaction to the ordeal by hurricane, the tussle with the sea-tossed mattress had been so vivid that Vatcher was quite unable to get to sleep again. He lay waiting for the dawn and wondering what sights it would bring with it.

It was a lovely dawn, a tourists' dream; but as the light quickened, the scene began to resemble a nightmare. Directly below the old gun position lay *Foundation Josephine*, the finest and proudest rescue ship in the western reaches of the ocean. But she did not look proud any more. She looked unbearably pathetic. She was listed outward to 20 degrees, and her exposed flank was ragged with the wounds made in it by the coral. Flung helpless on the land, her grace and beauty were all gone.

One by one her people roused, stood up and stared at her silently. These men, most of whose lives had been devoted to the rescue of ships, knew at a glance that *Josephine*—their vessel—was all but dead. They could see that she had been thrown in over a whole succession of coral reefs so that she was now all but land-locked. Even if her underwater wounds were not so severe as to doom her as a total loss, it seemed inconceivable that anything short of another hurricane could transport her back across those ledges into her own element.

It was at this juncture that Featherstone arrived on the scene for the second time. He had come back with Squires shortly after midnight, but there had been nothing to be done then and so, with his usual practicality, he had gone back to bed. In the morning he acquired a jeep from the Army base and drove to the tug through, around, and over the windrows of the wreckage. As he passed the air base at St. David's Island, he could see the crumpled shapes of aircraft on the landing field, and the grotesquely twisted radio towers. While coming along the shore road he had counted a score of roofless buildings. The road itself was littered with smashed palms and fallen telephone poles; and everywhere there was tattered and nameless debris to mark the serpent's track.

Jumping from the jeep, Featherstone strode over to the tug. His whole attention was concentrated on the stricken ship. For twenty minutes he climbed over her, peering into her holds and accommodations. When he finally came ashore his step was as brisk as ever and his face betrayed no sign of gloom.

"Big job," he said succinctly to the waiting men. "It'll take us a while. Now, what's happened to the *Leicester?*"

There was no immediate answer to that one. The whole sweep of Murray's Anchorage lay open to view, and there was no ship, and no sign of any ship in sight. On the distant reefs there was nothing but the white surf from the failing swells. *Leicester* had apparently vanished. But this was impossible. If she had gone down in those relatively shallow waters, her superstructure, or at least her spars, would have remained in sight. Yet there was nothing to be seen.

It was Ray Squires who solved the mystery. Ray had climbed to the high ground behind the little point where *Josephine* lay skewered, and idly glancing along the shore he saw a ship's topmasts apparently thrusting right out of the cliffs which lay on the north side of Whalebone Bay.

Squires' shout brought everyone up the hill, and a skein of wondering men was soon making its way around the foot of Whalebone Bay and out to the headland on the northern side.

They reached the edge of the cliff and there below them, driven hard ashore for her whole length, lay *Leicester*. She was not four hundred yards from *Josephine*, lying almost high and dry. Tucked comfortably against her shoreward flank was the battleship mooring which, along with its three concrete anchors, she had dragged to this quiet resting place.

At the time *Josephine* was torn away from her, *Leicester* still had one passenger aboard—an elderly coloured man who had been hired as night watchman. Now the morning rang to the shouts of the crewmen on the cliff as they tried to rouse some sign of life from the old man.

When their cries brought no response, they took to heaving largish rocks down the cliff and bouncing them off *Leicester's* plates. Still no response. Reluctantly, they gave the old man up for dead.

Later that morning Featherstone and some of the salvage gang boarded *Leicester* from a boat and proceeded to search the ship for the missing man. They found him—comfortably ensconced in the saloon where he had just made a pot of coffee. The watchman greeted his visitors with a broad smile and offered to share his coffee with them.

Even Featherstone was impressed by such sang-froid. Only it wasn't really sang-froid at all—it was acute deafness which accounted for the old man's casual manner. It was later discovered that he had not even realized he had been living through a hurricane aboard the derelict.

He had gone to bed early—about 1830 hours—and he had slept soundly until several hours later when, as he expressed it, he woke to feel some uneasy motions in the ship and to think to himself, "Lord Jesus, it must be rough out there tonight"—before drifting back into an old man's sleep once more.

When he was persuaded to come on deck and take a look around, his placidity deserted him. Horror-stricken, he immediately insisted on being put ashore, vowing that never again would he set foot upon a boat, "Not any kind of boat dere is!"

Leicester had suffered severely. Her rudder had been torn off; she was again listed to about 30 degrees; she had been holed in two of her holds and in several of her fuel tanks, and she had been thrown so high up on the shore that she lacked ten feet of water to ever float again.

"There was some pessimism around that morning," Featherstone remembers. "But I felt grateful we hadn't lost either of the ships and *Josie*'s crew as well, as we surely would have done if the wind had set them off shore onto the outer reefs. I knew I could refloat *Leicester* if all went well, and I had a pretty fair hunch that I could save the *Josie* too. The thing we had to do was to get to work."

PART TEN

Featherstone had lost a battle; but he had not yet lost the war. He began remobilizing his forces with the single-minded drive which was one of his hallmarks.

By 1000 hours on the 8th, he had roughed out plans to salvage both ships. He had put *Josie*'s crew to work removing that vessel's salvage equipment, and readying it for use. He had hired a new stevedoring gang. He had chartered a tug, and he had bewitched the British Admiralty into letting him borrow a floating derrick called the *Cyclops*.

He had also made arrangements to house *Josie*'s crew and the salvage gang in an ancient stone building that stood half hidden in a jungle of vegetation on nearby Coney Island. This building had once been a fever isolation hospital but for the past fifty years it had been abandoned to flying cockroaches, and to the lizards who warred on them.

Using a dory and a hired motor boat, the men moved their mattresses and blankets to the old building. The cook was provided with a coal-oil stove and this, together with some rudimentary galley gear salvaged from the tug, completed the domestic arrangements.

Everyone slept on the floor, and since there was only one even vaguely habitable room, the floor was crowded. Diver Tom Nolan found the congestion too much to bear, so he went snooping off through the jungle to see if he could find something a little more secluded. Next morning he confided to Ray Squires that he had indeed found a little house, just big enough for one man, and as private as anyone could wish. It even had what looked like a stone bed running right across the back of it.

Intrigued, Squires went with Nolan to have a look at this *cabaña* in the wilds.

"My God, Tom," said Squires when he saw it. "Do you know what this place is? It's the crematorium—where they used to burn the stiffs that died of yellow fever and the syphilis!"

That night Tom unobtrusively returned to the bosom of his friends in the main building.

Coney Island also produced something else of interest. This was *Josephine*'s starboard lifeboat which was found a mile from the nearest water and at least three miles from the spot in Murray's Anchorage where it had parted company with *Josephine*. The crash landing on Coney Island had reduced it to matchwood.

Featherstone's plane for refloating *Leicester* called for the use of ground tackle to heave the ship back into deep water once she had been lightened and her underwater damage repaired.

Ground tackle consists of one or more exceptionally large anchors dropped seaward of a stranded ship, and connected to the vessel's winches through a system of purchases made up of steel blocks and heavy wires. If the casualty has no power of her own, a shallow-draught tug is moored alongside to provide steam or electricity to run the winches.

In *Leicester's* case, Featherstone planned to use two eight-ton anchors, one of them placed 1500 feet off the bow and the other 2100 feet off the stern. By applying a strain alternately to the tackle on each anchor he hoped to be able to wiggle the big ship off the ground.

But first he had to lighten ship, and then repair her bottom damage.

There was no time for halfway measures. Early on the 8th the salvage gang slung stages over *Leicester*'s side, lowered oxyacetylene burning gear to the stages, and began cutting holes through the shell plating into the 'tweendeck spaces. Once these holes were opened, the labour gangs could begin shovelling the ballast down the sloping deck directly into the sea.

While this was going on, Diver Ray Squires began an

underwater inspection of the ship. He found that she was badly holed but there were few holes he could not plug, at least temporarily. He began taking measurements for patches.

Also that morning the tug st-10 placed the big salvage anchors in position. Ground-tackle wires were then run from them to *Leicester* where threefold purchases connected the wires to her winches.

By October 11th, some seven hundred tons of ballast had been shoved overboard. Ray Squires and Tom Nolan had fitted "soft patches" (of wood and canvas) to the worst of *Leicester*'s underwater wounds. Four big pumps had been mounted deep inside the ship and were ready to pit their capacity against the inflow from the myriad small leaks which could not be reached by the divers. The ground-tackle system had been set up taut and ready.

Early in the morning the pumps were started. st-10 was given a hawser from *Leicester*'s bow so she could add her bit to the general effort. As high water for the day approached, *Leicester*'s winches began to clank.

High water came. The ground-tackle wires were hove so taut that the winches could not gain another inch. st-10 surged on her hawser like a dog on a lead. The pumps roared in *Leicester*'s engine room and holds . . . and nothing happened. Ten thousand tons of stranded ship remained unmoving.

It was a disappointment to Featherstone, but not a totally unexpected one. He had realized that brute strength was going to have to play the major part in freeing *Leicester* and he knew how he could supplement the supply.

Lying in St. George's was the self-propelled bucket dredge *Cochrane* belonging to the island's government. This dredge was equipped with "spuds," steel pillars that can be cranked down until they reach sea bottom, where they firmly fix the dredge in place. The *Cochrane* had an immensely powerful winch fitted with a two-inch-diameter steel wire.

On the morning of the 12th the dredge steamed out to a position off *Leicester*'s bows. Her spuds were lowered and anchored, and her heavy steel cable was run to the stranded ship. At 1600 hours, on the evening tide, she took a strain in conjunction with the strain being exerted by the ground tackle. Almost imperceptibly, *Leicester's* head began to swing. She came inch by agonizing inch, crushing and grinding over the coral so slowly that, by the time the tide began to fall, her bows had only swung fifteen feet. Still, it was a start and a certain indication to Featherstone that he would eventually win.

Meanwhile, *Josephine* had not been totally neglected. The salvage gang had been carrying out a good deal of preliminary work attempting to plug some of her gaping underwater wounds. But the divers had been discovering more and more of these gashes, ranging from simple rivet holes to one which was twenty feet long and more than a foot wide.

She was so completely hemmed in by heads of coral and underwater boulders it proved impossible for the divers to get at the major wounds from the outside. Ray Squires attempted to work on some of them from inside the flooded ship. He spent many hours feeling his way painfully through the maze of obstructions in the pitch-black and flooded engine room, but he could not get enough room to manoeuvre patches and tools and eventually he had to give it up.

As the days passed, what little hope had been held for *Josephine's* survival faded. Her situation seemed almost hopeless when the noon plane on October 13th brought a stranger to Bermuda. His name was R. E. Chadwick and by vocation he was the President of the Foundation Company. But by avocation he was an ardent tugboat and salvage man. Chadwick had been receiving cabled reports from Featherstone and he was deeply concerned about *Foundation Josephine*. Not only was she a superb ship, but she was the very backbone of the Foundation fleet and totally irreplaceable under two years. Her loss would be a serious and perhaps crippling blow to Foundation Maritime. Chadwick had therefore determined to see for himself how bad the situation was, and to bring to bear upon the problem of refloating *Josephine* all his engineering skill and imaginative genius.

Chadwick had only two hours in which to make his examination before catching a plane for home. He therefore hired a taxi at the airport and instructed the driver to take him straight to the tug. It happened that there was no one aboard of her at that hour except Wally Myalls, who had never seen the Company President before.

"I was sitting on the starboard bulwarks having a smoke when this fellow hops out of a taxi and comes bowling down toward the boat. He was all dressed up like a bank manager and I didn't have any idea who the hell he was. He climbed aboard, threw me a look and says: 'You got a tape measure?'

"I thought he sure and hell had a nerve, but there was something in the way he stared at me that made me answer. I told him I had one.

"'Get it,' he says.

"He'd got me kind of interested by then, so I humoured him and got a fifty-foot steel tape.

"'Now,' he says, 'get me a boathook.'

"By this time I was sure he was a loony—probably a rich tourist who'd shook his nurse and was having an afternoon out. I got him the boathook.

"For the next hour he had me scrambling around that tug like I was a goat on a cliff. He measured every damn thing there was to measure. He stuck the boathook into places he couldn't get to himself, and then he measured *it*. And all the time he kept nodding his head and muttering away to himself.

"The taxi started to blow its horn—it was still waiting—and he looked at his watch and said:

"'Got to make that plane. Thanks for the hand. This is too good a boat to lose.' Then whoosh, he was gone."

Featherstone was quick to recognize the visitor from Wally's description. Recognition brought him no joy. For almost twenty years he and Chadwick had been waging a more or less amiable feud. Featherstone maintained that a knowledge of the sea and all its ways, combined with the instincts of a born seaman, were the prime requisites of a good salvage master; Chadwick was equally dogmatic in his own views.

This lightning visit by "the Chief" made it seem likely that Chadwick was about to involve himself in the salvage of the *Josephine*. If this happened, and particularly if Chadwick's efforts were successful, Featherstone's pride and reputation were bound to suffer.

October 15th turned out to be a bad all around for Featherstone.

During the afternoon an onshore wind began to blow. By 1600 hours it had reached gale proportions, forcing the cessation of all work on *Leicester* and threatening her with more underwater damage. Nor could any work be done on *Josephine*, for the seas were sweeping right across her decks.

To make things worse, the insurance underwriters chose this day to issue an ultimatum. They declared that they were not willing to go on paying daily hire to Foundation for the salvage of *Josephine*, and that the Company must either agree to a "No Cure—No Pay" Lloyd's Open Form Contract or the job would be given to an American salvage firm.

The mere prospect of having another company take a salvage job away from him, a job moreover which concerned a vessel of his own Company's fleet, was almost enough to give Featherstone apoplexy.

There was still more to come. At 2200 hours he received a cable from Montreal outlining Chadwick's personal plan for salvaging *Josephine*.

It was an imaginative conception, but risky, since it involved towing Foundation's biggest floating derrick, the *Scarboro*, all the way from Lake Ontario to Bermuda. The plan called first for the construction of a concrete fulcrum under *Josephine*'s mid-section. *Scarboro* was then to use her shear legs, which would take a 250-ton deadweight lift, to tip up the tug's stern and so enable the divers to reach and repair the major underwater damage. After that was done, *Scarboro* could use her powerful winches to haul the tug through, or over, the intervening reefs into deep water.

Featherstone's distaste for the project was only partly due to his awareness of the fact that *Scarboro*'s chances of surviving the long ocean tow would be slight indeed if she should encounter a storm en route. The real trouble with it was that it was Chadwick's plan.

On the morning of the 16th, strong northwest winds still persisted—but Featherstone could brook no further delays. He knew that the *Scarboro* would have already begun the descent of the St. Lawrence River. If he hoped to spike Chadwick's plan, he would have to refloat *Leicester* at once so that he would be free to apply all his energies to *Josephine*.

The pumps had almost mastered *Leicester*'s remaining leaks and another 200 tons of ballast had been jettisoned since the last attempts to get her off. Featherstone was optimistic as he gave the signal to begin a new attempt at noon on the 16th.

As the ground-tackle wires came taut *Leicester* began to move. Her head swung outward by about three degrees; but at this crucial moment one of the wires burst, and before it could be replaced the *Cochrane* reported that the heavy seas were damaging her spuds and that she must return to port. There was nothing for Featherstone to do but call off the operation. It was a bitter decision, for the next day was Sunday and, despite the urgency of the task, it was impossible to persuade the local people to work upon the Sabbath.

If the Bermudians couldn not work, however, the salvage men and *Josephine*'s crew could work double time. Featherstone herded them aboard the stranded ship and had them shovelling ballast all that long day through.

It was a task of which Buck Dassylva did not approve. And he not only refused to stir from the fever hospital, he armed himself with several large black bottles and prepared to enjoy the day of rest. He may have overdone it. Buck failed to appear during the three succeeding days.

On Wednesday Featherstone went in search of him and found him still on his bed, but with considerably fewer bottles by his side.

"Buck!" yelled Featherstone. "When in hell are you coming back to work?"

Buck sat up slowly, fixed the Salvage Master with a reproving if somewhat distant gaze and said indignantly:

"By Gar, capitan! You *know* I nevair work Sunday!"

It was not until 0700 hours on the morning of the 19th that *Leicester* finally began to slide clear of the coral reefs that had imprisoned her. It took the combined efforts of the *Cochrane*, two sets of ground tackle, and two chartered tugs to move her at all. She came extremely slowly; and twice she was hung up on underwater obstructions . . . but she came.

At 0900 hours she floated free and upright. But she still managed to give the tugs a hard time as they manoeuvred her out through the entrance to Murray's Anchorage and into St. George's Cut under the buffeting of a full southwest gale and heavy seas.

At 1030 hours the long struggle finally came to its conclusion and *Leicester* lay docilely moored alongside a dock in St. George's Harbour.

Featherstone detached a small group of his salvage men to prepare her for the tow onward to New York. These preparations consisted mainly of the application of concrete patches over the many holes and rents in her shell plating—patches which were applied from the inside and which could be expected to keep her reasonably free from leaks until she arrived in drydock. But the rest of Featherstone's crowd were already hard at work elsewhere.

CHAPTER 2

The completion of the *Leicester* job was somewhat marred for Featherstone by a cable from Chadwick:

> AUTHORIZE YOU SIGN LOF AGREEMENT
> JOSEPHINE STOP DISCONTINUE WORK ON
> HER PENDING ARRIVAL SCARBORO

As a consequence of this message Foundation Maritime was committed to a "No Cure—No Pay" contract for the salvage of its own tug. By any standards this looked like a long-odds gamble. Featherstone was used to gambling, but he saw no point in increasing the odds against success by delaying the attempt to free her until *Scarboro* arrived. Every new gale damaged the tug a little more, and made the ultimate refloating job more difficult. In any event, the Salvage Master was convinced that he could free her without the help of either *Scarboro* or Chadwick.

After reading the cable, he telephoned direct to Montreal demanding to be allowed to proceed with the job in his own way, pending the arrival of the *Scarboro*. He was a hard man to resist, and he eventually won permission. With that victory behind him, Featherstone got down to work in earnest.

In order to free *Josephine* it was first of all necessary that she be made to float again—not just at her normal waterline, but much higher still. This meant stripping her of everything that had any significant weight, and then patching her to the point where most of the water could be pumped out, or driven out through the use of compressed air.

During the afternoon of the 19th, two eight-inch sal-

vage pumps were put aboard *Josephine* and a salvage
gang began building level platforms for them on her slanting deck. While these were being installed, another gang
was at work sealing off as many of the tug's compartments and tanks as they could reach. At the same time
two divers worked in the flooded inwards of the vessel
to seal off other spaces such as the shaft tunnel and a
number of the ship's service tanks. Pressure hoses were
then run to these potential buoyancy chambers from a
pair of compressors which were landed on *Josephine's*
boat deck.

These were preliminary steps. The major task was the
closing of the gaping wounds in the flooded engine room.
Until this was accomplished, the ship could never be
made to float high enough to come over the surrounding
reefs.

This was the problem which had also faced Chadwick,
and which he had thought to solve by lifting the whole
stern of the ship clear of the ground so that divers could
get at the ripped and fractured bottom plates.

Featherstone had a different solution. Instead of lifting
the ship, he planned to roll her over on her starboard side.

At daylight on October 20th, he put the *Cochrane* in
position, four hundred yards to seaward, and ran her
winch wire to *Josephine*. Featherstone also ordered the
pumps and compressors to be started, and these managed
to remove sufficient water, and to inject sufficient air, to
raise the stern a few inches off the bottom. Then *Cochrane*
took the strain. Her two-inch wire came bar-taut and
Josephine rolled about three feet to starboard. It was
enough—though barely.

There was now just sufficient space under the engine
room to allow Nolan and Squires to wriggle in and apply
the necessary patches.

The weather seemed determined to give Featherstone
high blood pressure. Before work ceased on the evening of
the 20th, a northwest gale began to blow, and by midnight seas were again breaking right over *Josephine* and
threatening to wash the pumps and the air compressors
clean off her decks. Only some extremely risky work by

Bob Cooper and Buck Dassylva prevented this disaster from taking place. While the gale continued to blow all work had to be suspended.

The gale blew without abatement throughout the whole of the next day.

While Featherstone grew more and more impatient, his men philosophically took advantage of the holiday.

The salvors had found themselves becoming an increasingly fascinating attraction for the tourists who were now beginning to invade the island in large numbers. Herds of mainland gentlemen in bright shirts and broad straw hats took to gathering on the cliffs overlooking the stranded ships. They were often accompanied, and frequently outnumbered, by even more colourful coveys of female tourists whose admiration for the bronzed and brawny salvage men surpassed all bounds.

Some strange things happened. Amongst *Josephine*'s crew was a shy young technician from a Cape Breton village who, having been raised as an Oulde Kirk Scot should be, believed that women were the devil's chosen instruments. Unfortunately for him the tourist invasion included a statuesque blonde wench who thought the young technician was exactly what the doctor had ordered, and what the travel bureau had so far failed to provide.

As her interest became increasingly overt, the young technician became more and more harried. One night she picketed the *Leicester*, and the poor fellow did not dare to go ashore at all. That did him no good. During the small hours of the morning he was awakened by the rustle of silken garments and when he lit a match he found that the devil's most persistent acolyte had boarded the ship and was calmly preparing to slip into the bunk with him.

He is reputed to have fled down the anchor chain. It seems an unlikely story; although the Scots are a stubborn race.

In any event, it brought him only a brief respite. The lovely tourist became even more persistent. The young technician began to wear such a permanently haunted look that even the bemused salvage gang, who thought he must be mad to flee such a happy fate, began to feel sorry for him. One day the fugitive became so hard pressed that he begged to be allowed to don a diver's suit and join the underwater team. The diver to whom he put this request was reluctantly compelled to refuse it.

"Having saw that gal in action. I knowed it wouldn't do him any good. She'd have gone down after him. And with all that gear on, he never would have got away. I couldn't let it happen. The water was that clear we'd have had the whole damn salvage gang going over the side to watch the show."

While the young man fought his losing battle, the rest of the Foundation people accepted the adulation of the tourists with becoming modesty—and made the most of it. Featherstone might fume when the winds blew—but he was almost alone in his distress.

By the morning of October 22nd, Featherstone had had his fill of false starts and setbacks. He decided to refloat *Josephine* that day, come hell or high water.

"Cap had made up his mind all right," one of the salvage gang remembered, "and God help *Josephine*, us, and Bermuda too, if anything went wrong. His jaw was sticking out so far I thought he'd trip on it. I tell you, we went to work that day as if we meant it."

The divers were the first men on the job and shortly after dawn they were down patching new damage to the hull and renewing old patches which had come adrift during the storm. Dassylva and Cooper soon had the pumps and compressors dried out and in working order. The *Cochrane* steamed out and anchored herself in a predesignated spot. The tug sr-10 was standing by.

Featherstone had previously spent many hours sounding the shoals and reefs to seaward of *Josephine* but he had been able to find only one conceivable way to get her clear. This was through a natural passage between the coral heads and reefs. It was so narrow that in several places it was not as wide as *Josephine* herself.

By 1000 hours the tug was pumped as dry as possible

and every space aboard her which would hold air was
under pressure. Although still aground throughout most
of her length, she was as light as she would ever be. It
was time for the *Cochrane* to take a strain.

Cheered on by an audience of several hundred people
lining the nearby cliffs, *Cochrane* began to haul. It was a
harrowing process both to watch and to hear. *Josephine*
began to grind and shudder in her coral trough—but she
also began to move. At the end of an hour she had bull-
dozed her way about a hundred feet. Then, as her stern
came round and pointed to the open water, she became
immovably jammed between a series of coral heads.

At Featherstone's orders, st-10 put a heavy hawser on
the wreck's bows, and began fishtailing at full power.
This had the effect of pivoting *Josephine* back and forth
and grinding down the coral heads which blocked her
passage. It also had the effect of fracturing and damaging
her own plates but there was no other way to work her
clear.

At 1200 hours *Cochrane* again took the strain and *Josephine* began to move once more, bumping and lurching
over three more sets of reefs until, at 1220 hours, she
scraped over the last coral head and floated free.

She was free, but barely floating. Even as st-10 put her
towing warp on the big tug's bows and started her for
the naval dockyard near Hamilton, *Josephine* was beginning to settle noticeably deeper.

"All that was holding her up was the compressed air in
her compartments and tanks," Bob Cooper remembers.
"The pumps were losing ground all the time. If we'd lost
the compressors for just five minutes we'd have lost the
ship."

It was a full seven miles from the scene of the stranding
to the dockyards, and by the time the tow had progressed
halfway, *Josephine* lay so low in the water that st-10
could hardly keep her moving. At this critical juncture an
Admiralty tug came foaming up and made fast along
Josephine's starboard side. With this additional help, the
sinking tug was finally eased into the dockyard and made
fast to the breakwater.

If the tow from Whalebone Point to Ireland Island had brought considerable anxiety to the salvage men, it had driven Freddie, the ship's dog, to a near paroxysm of distress. Freddie had been living ashore with one of the Bermuda pilots while his ship lay on the ground. After his noon siesta on the 22nd, he had wandered down to pass the time of day with the salvage men—only to discover that his ship had put to sea without him.

Some of the bystanders attempted to explain that the tug was only going to Ireland Island, but Freddie was not to be soothed. With one deep bellow of despair he plunged into the sea and proceeded to demonstrate just what a Newfoundland dog could do when he put his mind to it.

He caught up with the tow five miles along the way.

"He didn't seem too tired," one of the men recalled. "But he was the maddest dog I ever see. For about two weeks he wouldn't trust nary a one of us, and he wouldn't come out of the saloon. He'd have bust himself for sure if some of the fellows hadn't brought a potted palm on board to help him out."

Foundation's contract for the second salvaging of the *Leicester* did not include delivery of the ship to the United States, since *Josephine* was unserviceable and *Lillian* was still involved with the *Oscar Chappell*. It was decided to charter the tug *Kevin Moran* to complete the tow. But Foundation provided a riding crew for *Leicester*, and this consisted of three of *Josephine's* Newfoundland crew members.

The prospect of riding a dead ship to New York was not particularly entrancing, nor was it improved by an incident which occurred on October 23rd. During this day the Chief of the St. George Police called on Featherstone.

"We've got a murderer on the loose, Captain," he said. "Feller broke out of jail last night. He'll probably try to get clear of the island and we have an idea he may stow away aboard your ship. Feller killed his chum with a butcher knife; but he probably didn't mean to do it. Tell your chaps to keep a sharp lookout. If he shows up they can tap him on the head and turn him over to the New York police."

Leicester sailed for New York at the end of the *Kevin Moran's* tow wire at noon on the 24th. During that day and the next the tow went well enough, averaging nearly six knots against a Force 5 wind. Being absolutely light, *Leicester* rode very high and presented a formidable expanse of ship for the wind to strike against, so that she tended to sheer badly. Nothing constructive could be done about this since she was minus her rudder, but Captain Leonard

Goodwin of the *Kevin Moran* was an old hand at towing dead ships.

The riding crew settled themselves comfortably in the saloon with a case of rum which had mysteriously appeared on board. At intervals of four hours all three men made an inspection; sounding the ship's wells to make sure she was not leaking, examining the towing line where it came over the vessel's bows for signs of chafing, and applying heavy grease to the fairlead to reduce this danger.

It was not strictly necessary for all three men to do this duty tour together; but if only one went, then he tended to feel lonely; and if two went, the man remaining in the saloon felt lonely. The mental image of a butcher knife hung over *Leicester* like the sword of Damocles.

There was another threat hanging over *Leicester* and this one was deadly real. On October 2nd, an area of low pressure had begun to develop about halfway between Bermuda and New York. Within twenty-four hours it had given birth to a major "extra-tropical" storm. It was not a cyclone. Nevertheless it was a formidable antagonist for any ship to encounter.

Two hours before midnight on the 25th, *Kevin Moran* and *Leicester* began to meet extremely heavy seas, and within an hour the wind had risen from the west to Force 8, full gale strength. The combined assault of wind and seas was so furious that the tow almost came to a standstill.

The storm grew worse during the early hours of the 26th, and Goodwin concluded that his only chance of saving *Leicester* was to keep her moving toward the lee of land. All through this day the *Kevin Moran* butted her way into a mountainous head sea, while the unwieldy bulk of the *Leicester* contested every mile of progress.

At noon on the 27th the *Kevin Moran* was still hanging onto her tow; but she was making such minute progress that it began to seem as if the 650-mile voyage to New York would last forever. It was a straight-forward slugging match between the tug and the wind and seas, with neither side gaining or giving any ground.

The riding crew began to forget about the escaped convict as *Leicester*, with no ballast to steady her, rolled and pitched with such violence that it became almost impossible for the men to keep their feet. She had also begun to "work" in an alarming manner, thereby threatening the temporary patches which had been put on in Bermuda. The riding crew were not greatly surprised when, on the morning of the 29th, they discovered that the water had begun to rise in several of her holds.

They watched the rise for three hours and then decided it was time to act. At 1300 hours the lookout on the *Kevin Moran* saw a distress rocket curve up from *Leicester's* bridge.

Captain Goodwin had already observed that *Leicester* had developed a new list of about 12 degrees. He therefore wasted no time in bringing the tow head to wind and in stopping the tug's engines while the mate and some of the crew launched a lifeboat.

As the riding crew abandoned ship down a rope ladder, two of them were washed off into the sea. Fortunately the boat was close alongside and they were quickly pulled to safety.

The riding crew reported to Goodwin that *Leicester* had fourteen feet of water in Number 5 hold, eight feet in Number 2, and that the water in the engine room was well above the floor plates.

The tow was then 270 miles due east of Cape Hatteras, having been driven nearly a hundred miles south of its intended course by the continuing gales. Considering *Leicester's* condition and the prevailing weather, Goodwin concluded that any attempt to get her to New York would probably doom her. He therefore set his course for the nearest port, Newport News, in the knowledge that if the worst came to the worst he might be able to drag the sinking ship into shallow water and beach her there.

The storm had now begun to shift northerly and by morning of the 30th the winds off Hatteras had fallen light.

Goodwin worked the speed of the tow up to seven knots, disregarding the terrific strain which this put on the towing wire. The possibility of bursting the wire had become the lesser of two evils.

At 1510 hours October 31st *Leicester* was eased into a secure berth at Newport News. Her travail was at end—this time for good.

She had been in jeopardy to seas and winds for six long weeks. Two hurricanes had worked their will on her. She had been cast ashore. And in running this final gamut, one of the worst storms of the winter season had nearly sent her to the bottom. Yet she had survived all these vicissitudes. It was as if the men who served and saved her had imbued her with something of their own enduring will to live, in the face of the implacable hostility of ancient Ocean and of the consuming Furies which rage within the Serpent's Coil.

AFTERMATH

Foundation Lillian's *voyage to the rescue of the* Oscar Chappell *was an epic in itself. Nine hundred miles east of Bermuda she was caught and severely mauled by Hurricane* IX. *During the remainder of her eastward passage she was plagued by engine trouble, but on October 14th she reached the casualty, connected up, and started for New York twenty-four hundred miles away. A thousand miles out of New York the tow ran into the same storm which had given Leicester and the Kevin Moran so much trouble; but Lillian held to her course and slugged it out. It was noon on November 5th before she raised Ambrose Light Ship off New York Harbour—and she then had one day's fuel left in her tanks.*

Having delivered her tow, she returned to Halifax. At long last the ship and her crew had a breather. It lasted just two weeks—and then they were off again, towing a floating dredge to West Africa.

Foundation Josephine *reached Halifax on November 18th, under tow. She went into drydock and remained there for three long months. It took an additional three months before she was again fit for sea. But when she sailed again, she became once more the foremost deep-sea rescue tug in North Atlantic waters, and she continued to uphold this reputation until late in 1952 when she was returned to the British Admiralty at their request. She is still afloat, still working, though no longer on commercial salvage service. Her place in Founda-*

tion's fleet has been taken by an able successor—the 3000-horsepower Foundation Vigilant.

Leicester *remained on dock in Baltimore until late November. In early December she was rejoined by Captain Lawson and nearly half of the original crew who had sailed her out of the Thames three months earlier. On December 14th she sailed from Baltimore to New York, reaching her destination on December 18th. It had taken her one hundred and five days to complete her ill-fated voyage from Tilbury.*

Leicester *did not remain with the Federal Steam Navigation Company. In September of 1950 she was sold to a Nassau firm and renamed* Inagua. *In 1958, she passed into the hands of a Panamanian company who renamed her* Serafin Topic.

Long-suffering but infinitely enduring, one of the few surviving Liberty vessels of her class which remains in service today, she is still afloat—still ploughing the waters of the world.

ABOUT THE AUTHOR

For nearly thirty years FARLEY MOWAT has written of the lands, seas and peoples of the Far North with a humor and raciness, an understanding and compassion that place him internationally among Canada's most distinguished authors.

Born in Belleville, Ontario in 1921, Mowat grew up in Belleville, Trenton, Windsor, Saskatoon, Toronto and Richmond Hill as his librarian father moved a household that included a miniature menagerie around the country; those early adventures were chronicled in *Owls in the Family* and *The Dog Who Wouldn't Be*. During World War II Mowat served in the army, entering as a private and emerging with the rank of captain. The experience of battle seared the imagination of the young soldier and gave rise to his most recent book, *And No Birds Sang*, a gripping eyewitness account of combat in Italy and Sicily.

Following his discharge, Mowat renewed his interest in the Canadian Arctic, an area he had first visited as a young man with an ornithologist uncle. Since 1949 he has lived in or visited almost every port of Canada and many other lands, including the distant regions of Siberia. He has said of himself, "I am a Northern Man . . . I like to think I am a reincarnation of the Norse saga men and, like them, my chief concern is with the tales of men, and other animals, living under conditions of natural adversity." His experiences have inspired such works as *People of the Deer, The Desperate People, Never Cry Wolf, A Whale for the Killing* and *The Boat Who Wouldn't Float*. Farley Mowat's twenty-five books have been published in over twenty languages in more than forty countries.